The Leader's Guide to Coaching and Mentoring

PEARSON

At Pearson, we believe in learning – all kinds of learning for all kinds of people. Whether it's at home, in the classroom or in the workplace, learning is the key to improving our life chances.

That's why we're working with leading authors to bring you the latest thinking and best practices, so you can get better at the things that are important to you. You can learn on the page or on the move, and with content that's always crafted to help you understand quickly and apply what you've learned.

If you want to upgrade your personal skills or accelerate your career, become a more effective leader or more powerful communicator, discover new opportunities or simply find more inspiration, we can help you make progress in your work and life.

Pearson is the world's leading learning company. Our portfolio includes the Financial Times and our education business, Pearson International.

Every day our work helps learning flourish, and wherever learning flourishes, so do people.

To learn more, please visit us at **www.pearson.com/uk**

The Financial Times

With a worldwide network of highly respected journalists, *The Financial Times* provides global business news, insightful opinion and expert analysis of business, finance and politics. With over 500 journalists reporting from 50 countries worldwide, our in-depth coverage of international news is objectively reported and analysed from an independent, global perspective.

To find out more, visit **www.ft.com/pearsonoffer/**

The Leader's Guide to Coaching and Mentoring

How to use soft skills to get
hard results

Mike Brent and Fiona Elsa Dent

Harlow, England • London • New York • Boston • San Francisco • Toronto • Sydney • Auckland • Singapore • Hong Kong
Tokyo • Seoul • Taipei • New Delhi • Cape Town • São Paulo • Mexico City • Madrid • Amsterdam • Munich • Paris • Milan

PEARSON EDUCATION LIMITED

Edinburgh Gate
Harlow CM20 2JE
United Kingdom
Tel: +44 (0)1279 623623
Web: www.pearson.com/uk

First edition published 2015 (print and electronic)
© Mike Brent and Fiona Elsa Dent 2015 (print and electronic)

ISBN: 978-1-292-07434-4 (print)
           978-1-292-07436-8 (PDF)
           978-1-292-07435-1 (eText)
           978-1-292-07437-5 (ePub)

British Library Cataloguing-in-Publication Data
A catalogue record for the print edition is available from the British Library

Library of Congress Cataloging-in-Publication Data
Brent, Mike.
   The leader's guide to coaching and mentoring : how to use soft skills to get
   hard results / Mike Brent and Fiona Elsa Dent.—1st Edition.
      pages cm
   Includes bibliographical references and index.
   ISBN 978-1-292-07434-4
   1. Employees—Coaching of. 2. Employees—Training of. I. Dent, Fiona Elsa.
   II. Title.
   HF5549.5.C53B74 2015
   658.3'124—dc23
                          2015024427

10 9 8 7 6 5 4 3 2 1
19 18 17 16 15

Print edition typeset in 9/13 and Melior Com Regular by 76
Print edition printed by Ashford Colour Press Ltd, Gosport

NOTE THAT ANY PAGE CROSS REFERENCES REFER TO THE
PRINT EDITION

Dedicated to the memory of two great coaches – the late Ian Vivyan Nash and the late Steve Watson and to our friend and colleague Richard Phillips who was an early supporter of coaching as a leadership and management skill.

Contents

part **5** Final thoughts

About the authors

Mike Brent is a Client and Programme Director at Ashridge Business School. He specialises in leadership, team building, influencing, coaching, cross-cultural management, leading change and personal development. His interests include how to foster self-awareness and creativity, and how to challenge effectively.

Mike has worked as a management trainer and consultant with many international companies, and has a particular interest in working with management teams. He has extensive international experience, having run seminars worldwide, including in Japan, China, Uzbekistan, Thailand, Malaysia, India, Indonesia, the US, Canada and South America.

Mike has published a number of articles and three books on influencing, coaching and leadership.

Fiona Elsa Dent is an independent trainer, executive coach and Associate at Ashridge Business School. Her previous experience was as Director of Executive Education at Ashridge, where she was part of the management team involved in setting the strategic direction of the organisation with a particular focus on human resources. She also managed programmes, client relationships, delivered management development solutions and coached leaders and managers.

Fiona has worked with a range of organisations and clients on a national and international basis, she continues to teach and consult across a broad range of leadership, personal, interpersonal and relationship skills.

Fiona has written nine books and continues to write and research in the areas of influence, relationship management, personal skills and women in business. For more information about Fiona, see her website: **www.feddevelopment.co.uk**

This is the fourth book Mike and Fiona have co-authored, two of which are also in the Leader's Guide series for Pearson Education: *The Leader's Guide to Influence* (2010) and *The Leader's Guide to Managing People* (2014).

Acknowledgements

We would like to express our appreciation to the many people who have contributed to our ideas and thoughts, in particular the managers and leaders we work with, who were willing to share their experiences and stories with us.

Particular thanks go to the following people: Steve Ridgley of the John Lewis Partnership, Kevin Bowring and Stuart Lancaster of the England Rugby Football Union, Nigel Melville CEO of USA Rugby, Kriss Akabusi, Simon Presswell, Mark McKergow, Dr Mark Lowther, Adrian Mclean and Richard Phillips.

Our colleagues at Ashridge are always supportive and in particular we offer thanks to Dr Carina Paine-Schofield, Sue Honore, Viki Holton, Professor Erik de Haan, Sharon West and all our colleagues in the Ashridge Library.

Finally, thanks to our publishers Pearson Education and in particular to our editors Nicole Eggleton and David Crosby.

Publisher's acknowledgements

We are grateful to the following for permission to reproduce copyright material:

Figure 3.3 adapted from Heron, J., *The Complete Facilitator's Handbook*, Kogan Page, 1999; figure 15.3 adapted from Jackson, P. Z. and McKergow, M., *The Solutions Focus: Making coaching and change simple*, Nicholas Brealey International, 2012, reproduced by kind permission of P. Z. Jackson and M. McKergow; figure 16.3 adapted from de Haan, E. and Burger, Y., *Coaching with Colleagues: An action guide for one to one learning*, Palgrave Macmillan, 2013; figure 25.1 adapted from Hawkins, P., *Leadership Team Coaching in Practice*, Kogan Page, 2014, reproduced courtesy of P. Hawkins.

In some instances we have been unable to trace the owners of copyright material, and we would appreciate any information that would enable us to do so.

Introduction and overview

Being an effective coach and/or mentor is now a critical skill in businesses and organisations and will set you apart as a leader and contribute to your success, credibility and reputation as a people manager. This book is aimed at any manager or executive who wants to incorporate coaching and mentoring into their day-to-day management and leadership.

We have drawn upon our own experience as people managers, leadership coaches and consultants in the field of leadership and people development. In addition to this we will refer to best practice in leadership, management, life and sports coaching all of which can offer assistance to anyone who wants to develop their skills and capabilities in these areas.

In many ways coaching and mentoring are about attitudes as well as skills, competences and capabilities. Some people are naturally skilled in this area, but many more feel they need help to become the best coach and/or mentor they can be. This book will help you to understand what's necessary to be a good coach and mentor and offers a variety of tips and techniques for success in a variety of coaching scenarios.

In Part 1 we will establish the fundamentals of coaching and mentoring, set out the case for coaching and put them into context as part of your leadership and management toolkit for effectiveness in today's complex and challenging business world. We will also examine personal approaches and styles of coaching to help you to assess your own approach and to develop a broader range of approaches, and finally we will offer suggestions for getting the most out of a coaching session.

In Part 2 we will explore a range of skills, capabilities and competences that are vital for success as a coach.

In Part 3 we will examine a range of approaches, models and tools that are regularly used when coaching others. We will explain how each process works and when it is appropriate and not appropriate.

In Part 4 we examine a variety of typical coaching scenarios and offer suggestions about the best strategies to adopt in each of the scenarios.

In Part 5 we draw together our final thoughts. We examine the idea of coaching supervision, and offer some tips for excellence and highlight traps to avoid.

part **1**

Coaching and mentoring fundamentals

In this opening part we introduce coaching and mentoring and explain what we mean by both concepts. We will also help you to think about your personal style and suggest ideas for how you can get the best out of your coaching and mentoring relationships and discussions.

Coaching in context

The essence of coaching is to use the wisdom of the coach to bring to consciousness the wisdom that those being coached hold within themselves.

David Clutterbuck (2007)

In this chapter we will explore what coaching is, why coaching is important, and look at how effective coaching is in practice. We will give a number of reasons why we think coaching is an important and essential part of the manager's toolkit, discuss the context of coaching and the barriers to implementing coaching in organisations.

What is coaching for managers?

Coaching for managers is different to the type of coaching practised by executive coaches. For example, their role in the organisation is to coach and nothing more. Typically an executive coach would not offer any advice, but the manager has to do many things, of which coaching is only one. They also have to instruct and teach and inform and offer guidance as well as coach. So the question becomes: *'When should I coach and when should I instruct?'*

So, what do we mean by coaching? Coaching is largely about listening to the other person and helping them to improve their effectiveness. There are a number of definitions of coaching. Eric Parsloe, Director of the Oxford School of Coaching and Mentoring, says that coaching is 'a process that enables learning and development to occur and thus performance to improve. To be a successful coach requires a knowledge and understanding of process as well as the variety of styles, skills and techniques that are appropriate to the context in which the coaching takes place.' Coaching expert Sir John Whitmore suggests that coaching is 'unblocking a person's potential to maximize their own performance. It is helping them to learn rather than teaching them.' We would wholeheartedly agree with both these definitions and add that it is about enabling people to think for themselves and come up with their own options and possibilities, rather than telling people what to do or just giving advice. When done well, coaching involves allowing your colleagues to develop their skills and knowledge to their full potential.

> Coaching involves allowing your colleagues to develop their skills and knowledge to their full potential

There are, however, many definitions of what coaching is. The UK's Chartered Institute of Personnel and Development (CIPD) acknowledges that there is a lack of clarity about exactly what coaching is and what it isn't – and how it differs, for example, from counselling and mentoring. We hope in this book to provide you with some clarity about the role of leaders and managers as coaches in today's business environment.

Why coach?

The art of coaching by line managers is becoming an essential part of the effective people leader's toolkit. There are a number of reasons for this:

▌ **Because we live in an increasingly complex world.** In the so-called VUCA world (Volatile, Uncertain, Complex and Ambiguous) there are fewer clear-cut solutions, so the need is for managers to use their people to develop more options and possibilities, rather than trying to give their own answer which may well be wrong and outdated. We will say more about this later in the book.

US President Barack Obama refers to the complexity of the world he is dealing with when he says in Mark Bowden's book *The Finish*: 'You're always dealing with probabilities. No issue comes to my desk that is perfectly solvable, because if people were absolutely certain, then it would have been decided by somebody else.'

▌ **To gain competitive advantage.** When products and services are similar, competitive advantage comes from having people with ideas, skills, responsibility and initiative. The core idea of coaching is to develop others, to help them learn and to instil confidence. Without coaching this cannot be achieved. Ultimately, as the environment grows more and more complex, performance will be as a result of learning. Writer and futurologist Alvin Toffler predicts the successful future organisation will be a learning organisation.

Reg Revans, the founder of Action Learning, used to say that if the environment changes faster than your organisation learns, you're out of business! Jack Welch, ex-CEO of General Electric, has also made this phrase his own. This means that we cannot wait for the rest of the organisation to change before we change. We have to take individual responsibility for learning, and as a people manager encourage others to do the same. Practising the art of coaching will help you to become an effective leader. In a conversation with Kevin Bowring, Head of Elite Coaching for the England Rugby Football Union, he told us that his colleague, Head Coach Stuart Lancaster, says that 'Coaches need to be open to learning and constantly learn themselves.'

▌ **Because expectations of Gen Y and Millennials have changed**. They expect managers to be coaches rather than directors who tell them what to do. In recent research undertaken at Ashridge Business School, 56 per cent of the Gen Y'rs surveyed identified that their ideal manager is someone who fulfils the role of coach or mentor. The disconnect is that 75 per cent of the managers who took part in the survey believe that they are fulfilling the role of coach/mentor while only 26 per cent of the Gen Y respondents think they actually do. Interestingly, more women (61 per cent) than men (48 per cent) want a coach/mentor relationship. Could this be a reflection of the preference among women for the more collaborative and cooperative approach to work and a willingness to embrace the emotional and self-awareness aspects of coaching? If this is the case it may mean that women are more accepting of the coaching approach and will more readily take on coaching roles.

▌ **To help people achieve**. Effective coaching is about helping people to achieve something they want to achieve, whether it be promotion, skills, improved performance, self-understanding or better balance. Coaching has to primarily focus on the individual being coached, in conjunction with the needs of the organisation.

▌ **To give others responsibility and ownership**. The aim of coaching is to produce better performance, whatever the field of coaching: sport, the arts or business.

People perform better and are more committed when they take responsibility and ownership for their actions. They can't do that if you are micromanaging them.

▌ **To develop your own skills as a leader.** Leadership entails taking a step back from the operational details of the job and looking more at the strategic and human elements. You won't be able to accomplish this if you are busy doing everything. Practising the art of coaching will help you to become an effective leader and will contribute to your organisational credibility and reputation.

▌ **To get people to think for themselves and develop initiative.** If you are the person who ends up having all the ideas then you are not encouraging your people to use their skills to the full. Your job is to develop your people, and that means getting them used to coming up with both new ideas and ways of implementing them. One of the most effective ways of doing this is to coach. As the saying goes: 'If we do what we always did, we will get what we always got.' So in the ever-changing and complex world in which we live, innovation and creativity are at a premium – your job is to encourage it in others, not just come up with all the ideas yourself.

▌ **Ownership.** The process of coaching people hands ownership of the issue back to the person being coached, who then is able to take responsibility for their actions and behaviours. You are more motivated if you have ownership. Solutions discovered by the coachee are more likely to be implemented on a sustainable basis than solutions imposed from above.

▌ **Autonomy.** If you coach someone rather than give him or her advice then you are effectively increasing their autonomy and showing you trust them, without abandoning them. According to Daniel Pink, in his book *Drive*, autonomy is one of the key engagers and motivators for individuals in organisations.

▌ **To support an organisation's mission, culture and values.**
Many organisations talk about the value of their people
and that they are their greatest asset. Coaching can
contribute to building on this part of any organisation's
mission or value statement by investing in the growth
and development of the staff. In a conversation with
Steve Ridgley, Coaching Manager at the John Lewis
Partnership, he talked about internal coaching as part
of the process of bringing about change in the culture
of the Partnership. In particular, he mentioned that
the skills and capabilities of an effective coach will
help to model the important need for open and honest
conversation as a way towards organisational excellence
and good interpersonal practice. At the John Lewis
Partnership coaching is linked to the organisation's
constitution, which is a written framework that defines
the Partnership's principles and the way it should
operate. In particular, Steve highlighted Principle 1 as
underpinning the Partnership's approach to coaching –
supporting Partners to find a satisfying and worthwhile
place in the organisation or broader happiness in their
lives. Principle 1 states: 'The Partnership's ultimate
purpose is the happiness of all its members, through
their worthwhile and satisfying employment in a
successful business. Because the Partnership is owned in
trust for its members, they share the responsibilities of
ownership as well as its rewards – profit, knowledge and
power.'

▌ **Creativity.** Coaching allows people to be more creative.
There isn't much scope for creativity if you are telling
people what to do. Your answer may not be as creative
or innovative as your colleagues. And creativity and
innovation are key differentiators in a VUCA world. Horst
Rittel and Melvin Webber, both professors in urban design
at the University of California in Berkeley, observed as

long ago as 1973 that problems could be divided into two types: 'Tame problems' and 'Wicked problems'. Tame problems, although they may be somewhat complex, can be resolved by applying established processes and techniques. Wicked problems, on the other hand, cannot be resolved in this way, and in fact have no right or wrong solutions – only better or worse, or good enough or not good enough.

Warwick Business School's Professor Keith Grint gives examples: a tame problem for example, is teaching your child to pass their driving test, a wicked problem is being and remaining a good parent to them. Clearly there are an unlimited number of wicked problems facing us today: from how to provide excellent health care, to the issues of drugs, terrorism, pollution and global warming to mention only a few. Most human and relational issues are wicked problems, in the sense that there are no obvious and clear answers to the issues like relationships, motivation, energy and dedication that managers have to face on a daily basis. Coaching is the ideal way to work in this VUCA world and to resolve wicked problems.

> The aim of coaching is to produce better performance

The context of manager as coach

Coaching someone is always going to be within a specific context. And the leader as coach has to be aware of the relationship and the different – and possibly competing – contexts within which he or she is operating. There are three aspects to the context as set out in Figure 1.1.

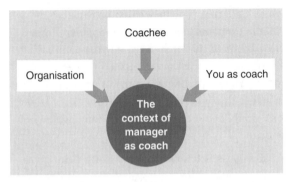

FIGURE 1.1 The context of manager as coach

The organisation context

The coach will need to be able to address the following questions:

▮ What are the current issues challenging the organisation?

▮ What is a coachee's perception of these?

▮ How are they affected by this context?

▮ How are they behaving?

▮ How might they behave differently within their team or department?

▮ What is the relationship between coachee and wider organisation?

▮ What is the relationship between coachee and the team?

These will all have an effect on each different coaching scenario or situation.

The coachee context

The coach will also need to be able to understand the context in which the coachee finds themselves. For instance:

▮ What are a coachee's values and attitudes?

▮ How does the coachee see things?

▮ What is happening for them?

▮ What are their perceptions and assumptions?

▮ What are their strengths?

▮ What are their development areas?

All of these will affect the coaching conversation.

Your context as a coach

Finally we need to look at you in context, as this will affect how you coach others:

▮ What is going on for you?

▮ What strengths, values and assumptions are you bringing to coaching?

▮ What is your relationship to the organisation?

▮ What is your relationship to the team?

▮ What is your relationship to the individual being coached?

All of the above have an influence on the coaching processes you adopt. Your answers to these questions will help you to become more aware of the context in which you are operating and will help you to determine your approach to any coaching situation.

Barriers to coaching

There are a number of barriers and hurdles that have been identified within organisations and among leaders and managers to using a coaching style and actively promoting coaching as part of their managerial philosophy. These are:

▌**Time.** We very often hear from managers that they would like to coach but simply don't have the time. For us this is a false problem. The reality is that managers don't have the time NOT to coach. Of course there is an investment of time up front, but if the result is that your people think for themselves, are creative and use their initiative, then ultimately you save time. And sometimes it takes less time to coach than it does to tell and convince someone that your way of doing things is indeed the right way.

▌**Reward.** It may be that leaders are not rewarded for coaching and developing their people. The organisation might not have built it into their reward structure, so any time spent coaching might be seen as a waste of time. The old adage that what gets rewarded gets done then comes into play.

▌**Competence.** Do leaders have the competence to coach effectively? We are not sure. We often see leaders who think they are coaching, but who are in fact telling people what to do and giving advice. Often they disguise their advice as coaching by framing it as a question. For example: 'Don't you think it would be a good idea to do. . .?' or 'Have you thought of. . .!' This isn't coaching! However, we do understand that leaders do need to give advice and offer ideas from time to time. Often it's a question of when to give the advice and we believe that any advice should be given after first of all questioning the coachee and raising their awareness of issues.

▌**Resources.** Does the leader or the organisation have the resources and will to train their managers to become coaches? Do they invest in training and coaching? Will they put in place an infrastructure and culture where coaching is simply the way things are done? If not, then it's likely that the initiative for coaching will die out.

▌ **Interest and motivation.** Does the leader have enough interest and motivation to actually coach as opposed to simply telling people what to do? Is the coaching mentality measured at recruitment? Is it rewarded (see above) formally or indeed informally? If a coaching approach is not part of the culture then employees might resist using the approach.

▌ **Culture.** The culture of the organisation could be a potential barrier to implementing coaching. If the culture of coaching within the organisation is autocratic and top down, then it is unlikely that a coaching culture could be easily implemented. There is a common expression in business that says 'culture eats strategy for breakfast'. In our experience the attitude of top management is critical. If they support coaching initiatives and actually use a coaching approach in their management style, then a coaching approach is more likely to succeed.

> The culture of the organisation could be a potential barrier to implementing coaching

▌ **Expertise.** Who is the expert? Traditionally leaders would say they are, and this leads to a bias in favour of telling and prescribing. We would challenge this perspective. The reality is that by definition a leader should rarely know more about a particular area than the person doing the job. The basis for promotion to management and leadership is often expertise in a specific area and so it's logical that when you get promoted you start to manage and lead in areas where you have no or little specific expertise. For example, many managers are promoted from specialist roles, such as Senior Marketing Manager to, say, Plant Director or Chief Operations Officer, so while they may have expertise in marketing they will not be an expert in any of the other areas reporting to them. For this expertise they will have to rely on others.

While this is often the case, there are undoubtedly times when the leader does have better knowledge or expertise than the person they are managing. But even then it is not evident that telling someone what to do and simply instructing them is the best way to proceed. The important question is: how can the leader with the greater functional expertise transfer knowledge in a sustainable way? Perhaps the manager can still coach by first finding out what the employee does know, or what ideas they might have before simply telling them what to do?

None of these barriers is insurmountable. However, it is important to be aware of them.

Is coaching effective?

If recent research is to be believed it would certainly seem that coaching is increasingly effective as a development process used by organisations. Of course, many organisations work with executive coaches. What we have experienced at Ashridge is that there is a growing trend to encourage leaders and managers to acquire and use coaching skills in their day-to-day role. In the Ridler Report published in 2013, *Trends in the Use of Executive Coaching*, respondents indicated that there was a clear trend towards the use of internal rather than external coaches.

Research by the UK's Corporate Executive Board in 2009, which is a leading member-based advisory company, found that coaching by an executive's manager drove leadership bench strength (this is a sports term which refers to the qualities and readiness of potential successors to move into key leadership positions) more than any other factor. The well-known Google organisation did some research in 2011 and they looked at the key indicators of successful managers and found that being a good coach was one of the indicators of effective management. For example they found that one to one coaching with a problem manager led to a 75 per cent improvement in that manager's performance. A recent survey by the CIPD shows that the key reason for organisations to coach was to improve performance and engagement. In conversation with Simon Presswell, an MD and entrepreneur in the music and entertainment business, he stressed that in the dynamic and ever-changing landscape of creative businesses, coaching can often act as a lighthouse warning of the impending danger of rocks ahead, and help you decide if you wish to avoid them. When the manager or leader acts as a coach they will be far more likely to pick up on the realities of their business situation.

> Coaching can often act as a lighthouse warning of the impending danger of rocks ahead

In fact the UK Chartered Institute of Personnel Development's annual survey on learning and talent development reports that coaching by line managers is ranked one of the most effective learning and talent development practices (CIPD 2013). Interestingly the same survey tells us that coaching is one of the key leadership skills that organisations lack! The fact is that many organisations are already using their managers and leaders as coaches. According to another CIPD report, more than 50 per cent of coaching in organisations is done by line managers and internal coaches (CIPD 2011). At Ashridge

Business School, training managers in coaching skills and techniques and offering qualification programmes for executive coaches has been a major part of their offering for many years. Professor Erik de Haan, Director of Ashridge's Centre for Coaching, suggests that coaching is:

▮ Based on the creation and maintenance of an effective working relationship.

▮ Focused on goals and outcomes while allowing creativity to emerge.

▮ Oriented towards successful organisational performance.

▮ An opportunity to offer individual feedback on perceived behaviour and styles in order to facilitate self-awareness, learning and personal change.

▮ Confidential.

It is clear to see that internal coaching by an organisation's own managers and leaders is fast becoming a major part of many organisation's learning and development strategy. In order for coaching to succeed in any organisation there must be a clear understanding of the benefits, challenges and barriers together with an organisational culture that supports, promotes and rewards coaching as a managerial philosophy.

Tips for success

▮ Remember, research shows that coaching leads to better performance.

▮ One of the main barriers to coaching is lack of time so you must actively make time to coach.

▮ The key to good coaching is good listening, so listen more than you speak.

▍ Remember, 'wicked' problems have options and
possibilities rather than definitive solutions.

▍ Your role as a coach is to help others learn for themselves
NOT to teach them.

▍ Generation Y expects and wants to be listened to and
coached.

▍ Coaching encourages independence in others.

Being a mentor

The delicate balance of mentoring someone is not creating them in your own image, but giving them the opportunity to create themselves.

Steven Spielberg, film director

Coaching and mentoring are often used synonymously, which can be confusing. A good mentor will use many of the same skills and techniques as a good coach, however in our view there are some key differences between a coach and a mentor. In this chapter we will explore these differences, why mentoring is an important role for managers and leaders, who you choose to mentor and the role of the mentor.

One of the most prolific writers and researchers in the area of mentoring (and to some extent coaching) is David Clutterbuck. He offers a couple of definitions of a mentor. One is 'Off-line help by one person to another in making significant transitions in knowledge, work or thinking', and the other is 'A mentor is a more experienced individual willing to share knowledge with someone less experienced in a relationship of mutual trust'. We particularly like the second definition as it captures the essence of what we believe mentoring to mean, although as you will see later in the book, less experienced people can also mentor or coach more experienced ones.

Mentoring is not a new concept. It can be dated back to Greek mythology and in particular to Homer's *Odyssey*. As the story goes, when King Odysseus went off to war he left his son Telemachus with his old friend Mentor, whom he considered to be a trusted paternal figure who could share his wisdom, knowledge and experience with Telemachus in his absence. The important thing about mentoring is the quality of the relationship. This needs to be one of complete trust and empathy, which then allows for honesty, openness and challenge between the two parties.

The important thing about mentoring is the quality of the relationship

In our view, and for the purposes of this book, a mentor is usually a more experienced person typically selected by the mentee for a variety of reasons:

- He or she is a more experienced person who they have worked with, admire and respect.
- He or she has a good track record of developing people.
- He or she is someone who is experienced in the organisation, profession or situation that the mentee feels can become a confidante and help them develop and grow.
- He or she is well connected and networked and can help the mentee develop and move ahead.

Mentoring relationships tend to be most successful when the choice of mentor rests with the mentee and almost always when the mentor is not the line manager. Some organisations are formalising mentoring as part of their HR policies and practices and encouraging leaders and managers to see mentoring as part of their role in the organisation. While this legitimises mentoring within the organisation, we still believe that it is most effective when the mentee plays a major role in selecting his or her mentor rather than being allocated a mentor. That said, when organisations do formalise the role, they often offer some training and this will of course be beneficial.

In a recent article in *Human Resource* magazine Virgin Group founder Richard Branson said: 'The spirit of mentoring should be embedded within UK businesses.' He suggests that a promising business person can become a successful business person with the aid of a mentor. 'Giving people advice and ideas on how to achieve their goals is often overlooked in British businesses.'

So how does mentoring differ from coaching? Some of the key differences are summarised below:

- When mentoring, the focus tends to be on career development or guidance and advice relating to the mentee's role.

- Most mentoring relationships are developed over a long period and can last for many years.

- There can be long periods of time between meetings.

- Meetings are often informal and impromptu and take place as and when needed by the mentee.

- Typically the mentor will be an older, more experienced colleague who knows the mentee and his/her profession and is willing to devote time to help in their development.

- A mentor will tend to react to the needs of the mentee to help them in their career development, sometimes offering advice and guidance.

CASE STUDY

Fiona has had three major mentoring relationships during her career in Management Training and Development. All three have been long term and only ended when she moved on from the organisation. The first relationship was with a colleague who was at the same level in the organisation but had many more years' experience in the role. The second, when she worked as a Management Development Manager was with a more senior manager in the organisation. Finally, her current mentor started as a colleague, became her boss and now works for an entirely different organisation – this is also the longest-term relationship. In all three cases the mentors were men and in some ways she feels this was beneficial given the balance of men and women in senior management and their assistance in helping her to understand the male perspective. The main role these people played in Fiona's career was to listen, challenge and on occasions offer advice and guidance based on their experience. The real success of these relationships was the non-judgemental nature of them and the ability for Fiona to be completely honest and open to share fears, worries and insecurities in order to face new challenges and take on new roles with increased confidence and self-belief. These three relationships differed significantly from the various coaching relationships Fiona has had. For her, coaching was more issue based, while mentoring tended to be rather more personal and holistically focused.

Being a mentor – why is it important?

A mentoring relationship will tend to be with someone more junior, probably younger and not within the mentor's line responsibility (this allows for a greater possibility of an open, honest and trusting relationship being developed). It is, of course, not impossible for a line manager to be a mentor, but it does add some boundary challenges to the situation – for instance, favouritism and impact on performance review situations. Taking on a mentoring role is a very serious commitment, and in addition to helping your mentee develop, you yourself will be developing your own skills and capabilities. As a mentor you will also be opening up new channels of communication for both yourself and the mentee that will give both of you access to different networks. It will also help you to be more aware of what other areas of the business are doing, thus gaining information and understanding about what's going on outside your normal relationship network in your organisation. Additionally it enables you to have the opportunity to challenge your own perspectives on various issues through the reflective process that you engage in with mentees.

Taking on a mentoring role is a very serious commitment

Both personally and organisationally it is important and beneficial to share your expertise, experience and wisdom with others so that they can learn from you. From an organisational perspective this is a cost-effective developmental approach as it is mentee driven and bureaucracy is kept to a minimum with little, if any, paperwork. It is real time and real life, and focuses on issues that are important to your mentee at a particular point in their lives. Because the mentee is mostly responsible for instigating and driving the relationship you will be certain to have a willing learner to work with.

As a mentor you can help your mentee to broaden their horizons and understand the overall strategic direction and goals of the organisation and to raise their awareness of the possibilities for career opportunities and progression. If you are in a senior management role and you have mentees, then it can make you aware of the talent in your organisation and can contribute to succession planning. Talent management and retention is a huge challenge for many organisations today. By encouraging mentoring relationships, both organisations and managers themselves build loyalty and help mentee's become empowered and motivated.

Who to mentor

The most successful mentoring relationships are those where the mentee has instigated the relationship or alternatively where the mentee has a choice of mentor. It is also best if you mentor people who are outside your normal working hierarchy. Mentoring relationships are most successful if you mentor someone who thinks differently to yourself and sees things through a different set of lenses. This allows for more breadth and learning in the relationship. Be wary of mentoring someone who is a friend as there will undoubtedly be issues of being completely honest when challenging each other.

> Be wary of mentoring someone who is a friend

Suggested ground rules for a mentoring relationship

Although mentoring tends to be a less formal process than coaching, mainly due to the voluntary nature of the relationship, it is still important to agree a way of working together. So, when you enter into a mentoring relationship with someone there are some key ground rules that are worth establishing at the beginning or early on in the process. These include:

▌ What are your expectations of each other?

▌ What are the mentee's goals and objectives?

▌ What sort of areas will the mentee wish to focus on – career development, current role, specific challenges, etc.?

▌ Who will take responsibility for setting up meetings, and their frequency? A good-quality mentoring relationship is usually driven by the mentee. The mentor will however have to make time available for the sessions.

▌ What level of formality do you expect? Usually the more informal the better with mentoring.

▌ How and when will you review how things are going?

▌ Are you going to keep notes? Sometimes brief notes to remind yourself of what was discussed are useful, but both parties must agree if this is the case.

▌ Agree the need for total confidentiality and respect for the integrity of the relationship. By this we mean that neither party should use the relationship in an exploitative way.

> A good-quality mentoring relationship is usually driven by the mentee

Mentoring is a brain to pick, an ear to listen, and a push in the right direction.

John C. Crosby, US politician

Tips for success

▌ Remember, mentoring is all about trust and empathy.

▌ Mentee's choose mentors, not the other way around.

▌ Mentoring involves sharing wisdom, experience and expertise to help with your mentee's career development and growth.

▌ React to your mentee's needs, not your own.

▌ Be open to learning about yourself through your role as mentor.

▌ It is best not to mentor direct reports.

▌ Confidentiality and absolute commitment to the relationship are key.

3

Identifying your personal coaching style

Most of you will have a preference in terms of the style you favour when coaching and it is valuable to know which style you tend to use the most. In addition to this it is important to recognise that while you may have a preference, coaching style is actually all about flexibility, adaptability and appropriateness. Good coaches will select their approach and style depending upon the person and the context rather than sticking rigidly to their preferred style. In this chapter we will help you identify your preference and introduce you to ideas for broadening, flexing and developing your style.

> Good coaches will select their approach and style depending upon the person and the context

Coaching style

In this context what we mean by coaching style is whether you have a tendency towards directional or relational coaching. For some of you the style you adopt may be connected to the topic or purpose of the coaching session, but for many people there is a tendency to veer towards one or the other approach.

▌ **Directional coaching.** This style of coaching is where you draw on your own experience to provide advice, guidance and direction to your coachee. You will be more comfortable using a structured approach to make suggestions, give guidance and offer solutions to the coachee.

▌ **Relational coaching.** This style of coaching is where you respond more to the person and work with the emotions and mood of the individual and situation. You will tend to be more exploratory in your approach and will help lead the coachee towards identifying their own solution.

The following inventory will help you to identify which approach you favour. Look at the two ends of the spectrum and assess what you believe to be your preference when coaching and developing others. Try to be as honest as possible – self-awareness about your natural approach will help you to understand where you wish to focus your development.

Look at the statements below and assess where you believe you sit on the spectrum.

So what does this analysis tell you? Do you tend to use more directive approaches or more relational approaches? Neither is right or wrong; rather both are appropriate depending upon the issue, situation and the person. The important thing with coaching style is to be aware of your tendencies and to recognise where you have strengths and where you might wish to develop. In order to be a truly effective leader or manager as coach in today's business world versatility is critically important.

Coaching style quiz

A TENDENCY TOWARDS DIRECTIVE BEHAVIOUR	Indicate on the line where you would place yourself in relation to your natural tendency when coaching _____X_____	A TENDENCY TOWARDS RELATIONAL BEHAVIOUR
Taking responsibility for setting the agenda and focus of the discussion		Asking the coachee to establish the focus and agenda for the session
Advising about the situation/topic		Probing to determine the topic and focus of the session
Giving guidance for the way ahead		Assessing the emotional state of the coachee
Setting objectives and milestones for others to achieve		Asking the coachee how they know they will have been successful
Telling the coachee what their strategy should be		Working together to build a strategy
Focusing on issues and ideas		Focusing on feelings and emotions
Asking focused questions about what's been achieved so far		Probing to determine the full extent of the issue
Tendency to speak and offer advice more than listening		Tendency to ask questions and listen fully to the coachee about the issue
Relying on your expertise, authority and experience to help your coachee		Using your interpersonal skills as a major element of your coaching skill

The following model summarises some of the key skills associated with coaching styles. Some of these skills tend towards the directive while others are more relational or facilitative. Sometimes it will actually depend upon how you use the style as to whether you are veering towards directive or non-directive coaching.

When might you use these approaches? Obviously each coaching issue and each person you coach is different, so much will depend upon the situation you are faced with, together with your personal knowledge about the needs of the person you are coaching. However, one rule of thumb you may wish to apply is based on a model originally developed by Ralph Stacey (1996) which suggests that in today's business world we are faced with challenges that can be categorised into four areas – simple, complicated, complex and chaotic.

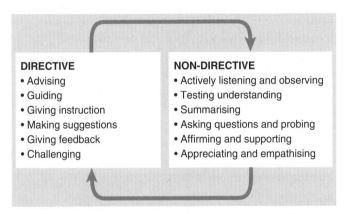

DIRECTIVE
- Advising
- Guiding
- Giving instruction
- Making suggestions
- Giving feedback
- Challenging

NON-DIRECTIVE
- Actively listening and observing
- Testing understanding
- Summarising
- Asking questions and probing
- Affirming and supporting
- Appreciating and empathising

FIGURE 3.1 Directive vs non-directive coaching style

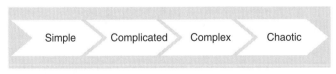

Simple Complicated Complex Chaotic

FIGURE 3.2 Contemporary business challenges

Simple challenges are a bit like puzzles where there are specific outcomes and processes for getting to these outcomes (a bit like a crossword puzzle or Sudoku) where the answer is known. The answer is known by someone and if you, the coach, are that someone then you probably want to adopt a more directive approach, perhaps offering suggestions, guidance or advice as part of your coaching discussion.

Complicated challenges are a bit more challenging where there isn't one definite answer but where more is known than unknown. Experience of similar situations may suggest ideas for what works and what doesn't, so perhaps a combination of directive with some facilitative approaches should be used to encourage exploration of the range of possibilities.

Complex challenges are a much more frequent part of most of our lives today where more is unknown than known. Such situations are where there is no one definitive answer, often experienced in times of change. In fact there are many possibilities based on an individual's knowledge, experience, motivation and commitment. When dealing with these often highly complex and ambiguous situations you probably need to use more facilitative approaches. It will be important to understand the full extent of the issue and to encourage your coachee to look at the issue in different ways. This will ensure that they are considering as many different facets as possible to help them get to the most appropriate course of action and outcome.

Chaotic challenges arise when a situation is highly confused and uncertain, and where there are lots of different opinions and ideas, but there is no correct answer – only better or worse options. Very little is known in this type of situation. Such situations will demand patience and skill on the part of the coach to work with them in a non-directive way. When a coachee is faced with a chaotic situation they are often seeking reassurance and an opportunity to explore with someone who has time and the energy to work with them. They probably do not expect answers, but what they do want is the opportunity to think together about the situation and perhaps receive both support for new ideas and also challenges to force them to broaden their ideas in order to help them clarify their values, assumptions, needs and energy. An example here might be where people are making big career changes or choices.

One further approach that could help you reflect about your personal coaching style is Heron's Six Categories of Intervention, first developed by John Heron in the 1970s. He identified two basic styles that he called authoritative and facilitative, and within each style he suggested that there were different intervention approaches you could use:

▌ Authoritative – prescriptive, informative, confronting.

▌ Facilitative – cathartic, catalytic, supportive.

At Ashridge we have worked extensively with this model and used it as an approach to help in both our own and others' coaching practices. We have also adapted the model, without losing any of its original integrity, to make the language more relevant to practising managers.

Coaching styles

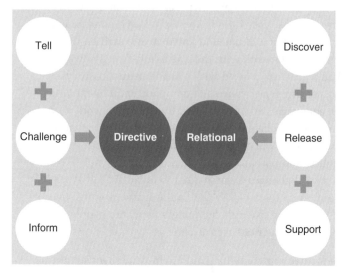

FIGURE 3.3 Directive and relational coaching styles

Source: adapted from Heron, J., *The Complete Facilitator's Handbook* (Kogan Page, 1999)

Each of these styles has its own purpose and process and the table below summarises this:

TABLE 3.1 Coaching style – purpose and process

DIRECTIVE	
TELL	**Purpose:** mainly used with people who lack confidence or self-belief and who need direction **Process:** give clear instructions and explain why they are doing something to ensure full understanding
CHALLENGE	**Purpose:** to encourage your coachee to challenge their assumptions and perceptions **Process:** ask questions, encourage reflection and give feedback
INFORM	**Purpose:** to share ideas or experience **Process:** present your ideas or share your experience making sure the coachee understands by asking them to summarise

RELATIONAL	
DISCOVER	**Purpose:** to take your coachee to a greater level of understanding and to promote commitment to and responsibility for actions **Process:** Lots of open questions, reflecting and silence to encourage the coachee to discover for themselves
RELEASE	**Purpose:** to encourage the coachee to share any emotional responses to a situation **Process:** support and empathise while listening and questioning to encourage emotions to be shared and dissipated
SUPPORT	**Purpose:** to develop self-confidence and self-belief and to encourage more learning **Process:** use appreciative and affirming feedback and ask questions to ensure the coachee fully understands

You may find it useful to reflect about your own natural approach to coaching and use this model to help you understand your preferences and tendencies, and to highlight where you could develop new approaches. One way of doing this is to assess your comfort and capability in using each of the styles (see Table 3.2).

Should you wish to examine your style in further detail you may find it useful to complete a more detailed questionnaire. Ashridge Business School has recently developed a Coaching

TABLE 3.2 Coaching style – self-analysis exercise

COACHING STYLE SELF-ANALYSIS EXERCISE

Allocate 30 points between the 6 styles with the highest number representing the style you feel most reflects your style to the lowest number representing your least preferred style

DIRECTIVE			RELATIONAL		
Tell	Challenge	Inform	Discover	Release	Support

Behaviours Questionnaire that could help you and is available through Ashridge Psychometrics (**psychometrics@ashridge.org.uk**). Other questionnaires which are available on the internet include the 'Leadership and Coaching Styles Questionnaire' at **www.stepchangedevelopment.com** and the 'Coaching Style Inventory' at **www.castletonconsulting.co.uk.**

As a leader or manager who is committed to coaching as part of their approach to working with others, it will be important to get to grips with a wide range of skills and approaches. The exercises and models above should provide you with an initial way of thinking about your preferences, capabilities and development needs. In the chapters that follow we will explore some of the main skills, approaches and processes that will help you to succeed in this area. We will also examine some common coaching situations and offer suggestions and ideas for dealing with them.

> It will be important to get to grips with a wide range of skills and approaches

Tips for success

- Know your own style and strengths as a coach.
- Use a style that suits you, the coachee and the situation.
- Ask for feedback about your style and its appropriateness.
- You may need to use several different styles during any one coaching session depending on the range of topics discussed.
- Work to develop versatility and flexibility in your style.

Getting the most out of a coaching session

The purpose of the contract is to ensure an effective, hassle free relationship and, like any contract, you do not need it until you do.

Myles Downey, writer and coach

To get the best out of any coaching relationship it is important for the coach and coachee to have an initial exploratory discussion or meeting where they will have the opportunity to begin to build their relationship, establish ground rules, and to identify goals and outcomes for their coaching relationship and sessions. This initial meeting is beneficial for both the coach and coachee and is often referred to as a contracting meeting.

Contracting

Some degree of contracting is important even if you are the line manager of your coachee, and even more important if your coachee is a manager within the organisation who is not yet known to you. The information that follows summarises guidance that will be useful to any person who is taking on a coaching role; however, you will have to adapt what and how you do it to suit the particular situation you are in.

The contracting process is essentially an opportunity for both parties to agree and understand each other's expectations and to establish ground rules and ways of working. These 'contracts' can be formal or informal as is appropriate for the people involved. They can be verbal or written, again depending upon the people involved. The complexity of any contract will tend to reflect the projected depth, frequency and formality of the actual coaching relationship.

> Understand each other's expectations and establish ground rules and ways of working

Benefits

The main benefits of this introductory meeting and contracting (especially if you do not already know one another) include:

- An opportunity to get to know one another and to decide if you are suited for a coaching relationship.

- Clarity on both sides regarding expectations.

- Discussion between both parties about style and approach for the coaching sessions.

- An understanding about the desired outcomes for the coaching relationship.

- A chance to agree the basis for reviewing the coaching process.

- Time to deal with the basic administrative issues – session duration, venue, cancellation or postponement of session policy.

- A discussion and clarification of ethical and confidentiality issues. This is particularly important when line managers take on a coaching role.

Formal or informal

One of the first decisions you will have to make is whether to have a formal or informal 'contract'. One of the main differences is whether the contract is written or verbal.

A written contract makes the whole process more official and enables both parties to sign up to the ethical aspects of coaching together with the practicalities of process and the administrative issues. Writing everything down and having both people sign up to this agreement creates a more formal relationship between the coach and coachee. Formal contracts are most beneficial when the relationship is part of an official organisational process. The written contract also gives you both a document that can be referred back to as part of the review process during the coaching relationship. This is more likely to be used when you are coaching someone who is not a direct report.

A written contract makes the whole process more official

A less formal agreement involves a simple verbal discussion during the initial meeting. This discussion will cover many of the same issues as a written agreement would cover – ethics, practicalities, goals and outcomes and the general ground rules. This type of agreement is typically used when the relationship is less formal and possibly based around a specific issue rather than an on-going long-term relationship. You would be more likely to use an informal agreement when you are coaching a direct report.

Some people use a combination of both the formal and informal approach. This would be a short formal written contract regarding ethics, and expectations on both sides followed by a less formal verbal agreement relating to style, specific session objectives and timing.

Ground rules – the important issues

▌ **Introductions.** Start by building rapport. The coach should talk about their background and experience, any qualifications and perhaps a little about why they enjoy coaching others. The coachee should be encouraged to talk about their understanding of coaching, their current role, as much about their background as they feel comfortable sharing at this stage (we find it useful to ask coachees to share a brief CV) and why they think coaching is for them.

▌ **What coaching involves.** Explore together your understanding of the coaching process. You may wish to discuss style here, and what your coachee expects from a coaching relationship with you, which may of course be informed by some previous experience of coaching. During this discussion you should also focus on:

– **The coach's role** – what you see your role as and what it's not. Coaches tend to talk about their role in listening, questioning, supporting, challenging and giving feedback to help people work through problems and issues in a structured and organised manner. Some coaching situations may involve the coach offering ideas or suggestions to explore together as a possible way to move ahead. What the coach won't be able to do is solve the problem or give the coachee the answers. As a coach you should always review each session to ensure that you are both satisfied with the process and progress.

– **The coachee's role** – when you enter a coaching relationship it is important that the coachee is open to change and challenge: this is the main purpose of coaching. The coachee must be willing to share problems and issues with you who will question and probe to help examine the full extent of the issue/s. During this process the coachee should expect to be challenged and to be given feedback in relation to the issue or problem. It is also the coachee's responsibility to work with the coach to develop an action plan and then to implement this plan. For a coaching relationship to be truly successful, commitment to action is necessary – no one else can do it for them.

▌ **Process and administrative issues.** There are several practicalities that need to be established in order for any coaching relationship to be effective and successful. These fall into seven key areas:

– *Ethics and confidentiality*. The coaching relationship is built on the basis of mutual respect and trust on both sides. Any topic of discussion or materials used during the process should remain confidential between the coach and coachee.

The coaching relationship is built on the basis of mutual respect and trust

– *Ground rules regarding the meeting process*. Listen non-judgementally, encourage full exploration of problems and issues through questions and challenge, provide constructive and honest feedback and encourage the coachee towards an action plan.

– *Timing*. Specifically duration and frequency of meetings. Much will depend upon the coachee's needs. Occasionally one or two short meetings (45 to 60 minutes) are all that is necessary, while with other clients a longer relationship with more in-depth meetings will be required. Typically two hours is the maximum time dedicated to any one meeting – the concentration level required for good-quality coaching is difficult to maintain for longer than this period.

– *Venue.* The most important issue here is to meet somewhere that you are both comfortable – an office, meeting room or sometimes people prefer to meet away from their place of work in a quiet corner in a coffee shop or the local library, or similarly quiet venue.

– *Note taking.* Both the coach and coachee should be encouraged to take notes or record the session. The purpose of notes is to capture the essence of the session and to summarise any actions agreed. They should be very brief to avoid getting in the way of the flow of communication. They are beneficial especially in a long-term coaching relationship to ensure progress is made and to remind you of the process so far. As a coach you should always ask for permission from your coachee and also be prepared to show them to the coachee if requested. They should NEVER be shared with anyone else.

– *Cancellation.* During this early meeting it is important to establish how you will deal with any cancellation of scheduled meetings. Be clear that cancellation should only occur in extreme circumstances – repeated cancellation may indicate lack of commitment to the issue, to coaching in general or problems in the relationship.

– *Concluding the relationship.* Even the best coaching relationships come to a close. Whatever the reason for the conclusion of the relationship good endings are important. They might involve any or all of the following:

  ● summarise what you have achieved together
  ● agree any final actions
  ● review the process and discuss what worked and what could have been done differently
  ● offer appreciative feedback to each other.

Using these guidelines will help you to get the best out of any coaching relationship. However, you will have to adapt and flex them to suit your own situation and the relationship you are developing.

Tips for success

▌ In any coaching relationship take time to contract about the rules of the road.

▌ At this contracting meeting you must:

— explore whether the relationship will work

— build rapport

— agree the basic process to be adopted

— agree any practicalities – timing, venue, note taking, etc.

— talk about your style

— make your coachee aware that coaching is about helping them solve their own problems, not you giving them answers.

▌ Ensure your coachee is both open to challenge and committed to action.

2
Part

Coaching and mentoring skills

In this part we will examine a range of skills that we consider to be the most important skills for any coach or mentor to have in their repertoire and to be able to use in a competent and capable way.

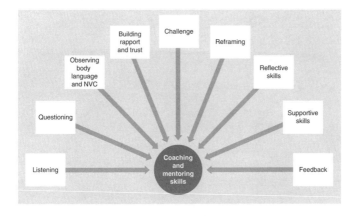

Listening

A good leader is a good listener.

Martin Whitmarsh, CEO of McLaren Group

L istening is clearly a key skill for success in any coaching relationship. Effective coaches must be able to listen more and listen better than the average person, and in this short chapter we will give you some ideas and tips on how to become a more effective listener. As a coach you will be using a technique called active listening. This is a technique that is used a lot in the helping professions where it is important to demonstrate that you have heard the other person. It means that you are able to focus on exactly what the coachee says AND also how he/she says it.

Effective coaches must be able to listen more and listen better than the average person

How to listen actively

Research shows that the following behaviours increase and demonstrate active listening:

▌ **Concentrate on the other person and don't daydream.** Your focus is on the coachee so you need to clear your head of any thoughts and concerns you are having and be in the here and now.

▌ **Defer any judgement.** It is natural to have your own opinions and judgements. But it's not helpful to share your judgement with your coachee. Remember that firstly your judgement may be inaccurate and, secondly, if you are judgemental it will get in the way of the coaching process.

▌ **Pay attention to the paralinguistics.** Note, for example, the tone of voice. Check the body language for cues and clues about emotions and feelings in relation to the issue. We have written about this in more detail in Chapter 7.

▌ **Just relax and listen.** Don't try to anticipate your next question or try to solve the coachee's issues.

▌ **Don't interrupt.** Interruptions will block the coachee's train of thought and, apart from anything else, it is rude.

▌ **Match and mirror body language – your vocal usage and general demeanour should be in harmony with your coachee's behaviour.** So, for instance, if your coachee speaks softly and slowly you should take account of this and adapt your voice and pace accordingly. What you must take care NOT to do is to mimic.

▌ **Maintain good-quality eye contact.** Look at the other person directly and lean slightly forward towards them. This will show that you are interested in and attentive to the coachee. Try not to sit directly opposite but at a slight angle so that the coachee can actually see that you are paying attention.

▌ **Don't make assumptions about your coachee or their situation.** For instance, don't say, *'I know exactly what you mean.'* You probably don't!

▌ **Show your interest by acknowledging the other person's comments by nodding, smiling and having a relaxed facial expression.** Giving your coachee a blank stare is not going to be helpful to elicit trust and encourage good communication.

Levels of listening

One tool that we often use at Ashridge is something called Levels of Listening. As its name suggests, we can listen on different levels. For example, we are often very good at listening for the facts of a situation, but less so at listening for the emotions involved. At a deeper level we could mention that there are intentions and assumptions behind what people say, so how do we listen in order to find out what these intentions and assumptions are?

▌ We can listen on different levels

When training people to develop coaching skills we use an exercise to demonstrate the complexity of active listening. The process we use is:

▌ Work in groups of five.

▌ Ask one person to speak for a few minutes on an unresolved issue they feel strongly about.

▌ Ask the others in the group not to interrupt or ask questions but to listen at different levels.

▌ Remember, each person listens at a different level.

▌ Once the speaker has finished, ensure the listeners offer them feedback on what they have heard.

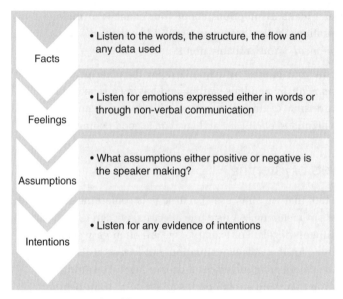

FIGURE 5.1 Levels of listening

From a listening perspective the lessons gained from this exercise are:

▊ Listening at more than one or two levels is difficult.

▊ Often people find that they identify their preference; some find factual listening easy while others find the feelings level easier.

▊ Many people find the factual level quite simple.

▊ Listening for emotions is usually far more challenging especially as these are more likely to be revealed in the facial expressions, paralinguistics and body language (see Chapter 7).

▊ Listening for intentions and assumptions is even more difficult, but if you are fully present, listening actively and are looking out for intentions and assumptions, then you will find it becomes easier. The idea is not to be able to tell someone what their assumptions or intentions are, but rather to be able to ask good questions about them.

Listening at the different levels helps you as a coach to listen not only to what is being said, but to what is NOT being said – this can often be more important than the words actually spoken. A good coach will develop their ability to listen at all levels. As a manager or leader you should hone this skill in many different situations so that when coaching it comes more naturally.

> A good coach will develop their ability to listen at all levels

As an example of how difficult it can be to listen effectively we would like to share something that happened to Mike during one of his sessions. A female participant asked one of the male participants how he felt about a particular issue. He responded by saying, 'Well what I think is. . .' and then expounded at great length on what he thought. His partner then gently asked him exactly the same question again. To which he replied – this time with some frustration – 'Well what I think, as I've already said, is . . .' When he had finished, his partner once again asked him how he felt. Given that the male participant was clearly not getting it, Mike intervened and pointed out that he had been asked how he felt and not what he thought!

Barriers to listening

There are several barriers to effective listening. Some of them are external, such as noise or interruptions, but the key barriers are internal ones – not really being interested in the other person, for instance, or being preoccupied with your own stuff, or listening in order to counteract the other person's perspective. The trick is to clear your mind, focus your attention and simply listen to the other person and not listen to yourself. Unfortunately it's not as easy as it sounds. As American psychologist Carl Rogers said: 'The tendency to react to any emotionally meaningful statement by forming an evaluation of it from our own perspective is the major barrier to interpersonal communication.'

> The key barriers are internal ones

Of all the skills for coaching and mentoring, listening (together with questioning) is one of the two most important. Poor listening ability or selective listening will hamper your coaching effectiveness and will affect the quality of your relationship, and even your reputation as a coach.

Developing and practising your active listening skills is time well spent.

Tips for success

- Coaching involves listening more than speaking.
- Before any coaching session, clear your head of thoughts and focus on your coachee.
- Listen for emotions, assumptions and intentions as well as the facts.
- Rephrase what your coachee has said from time to time, to ensure you have understood and to demonstrate good listening.
- Question for understanding when necessary.
- Practise listening at different levels with your friends and colleagues.

6 Questioning

If I had an hour to solve a problem and my life depended on the solution, I would spend the first 55 minutes determining the proper question to ask, for once I know the proper question, I could solve the problem in less than 5 minutes.

Einstein

Questioning, along with listening, are critical skills for coaching. As a coach you need to inquire and probe to allow the coachee to discover more, become more aware, and work out answers for themselves.

Asking good questions isn't easy. We find that people tend to tell and give advice rather than think of the right question to ask. The humanist psychologist Carl Rogers tells us that our inability to communicate is a result of our failure to listen and respond effectively. So it is very important for a coach to set aside his or her natural tendency to give advice and to focus on inquiry by asking good questions and actively listening to the answers.

> As a coach you need to inquire and probe

"CLEAN"

So what is a good question? A good question is one that does not make assumptions or judgements, either in the way it is framed or in the tone in which it is asked.

Many questions are not actually questions but are just displaced statements, or worse still, accusations. We often make judgements and assumptions about what the other person is saying and this stops us from truly listening. We need to suspend these judgements and assumptions. So, a good question is one that:

▍ Encourages reflection and makes the coachee truly reflect on the situation. It obliges the coachee to look at an issue from different perspectives. Good reflective questions encourage the coachee to think more deeply and broadly about their issue or situation. (See Chapter 10 for more on reflective skills.)

▍ Encourages the coachee to focus on what they can do and develop solutions rather than focusing on blame, excuses or constantly going over old ground.

▍ Allows enough time for the coachee to answer questions. It is very important that once you have asked a question, you remain silent and allow the coachee to reflect then answer. We often see managers asking coaching questions, then another then another. Or sometimes even answering their own questions! It's as if they are afraid of being quiet for a moment, but if they don't remain silent then there is no opportunity for the coachee to think and answer. So ask a question and leave space – in other words, shut up! This can be very hard for extraverted coaches especially if they are coaching introverted people who might take a long time to reflect before they answer.

▍ Does not betray or give away your own perspective or answer to the issue. It is very easy when asking a question to allow your own perspective to creep into the structure of your question and lead the coachee. Coaching is all about encouraging the coachee to develop the solution for themselves.

▌ Challenges people to question their own assumptions. Sometimes we presume things that aren't really true – a coach's job is to listen for, question and challenge any assumptions.

▌ Allows a person to express both emotions and facts. Typically managers are good at asking questions about facts. They want to know the facts, probably so that they can solve the problem. But the coach's job is not to solve the problem, but to make the coachee more aware and come up with options and possibilities, and not the answer. As a coach you probably need to ask more questions about emotions and feelings. People are often concerned that it's not appropriate to ask about feelings, but emotions more than facts determine what someone might actually do. So ask the coachee how they feel. Ask them how the other people involved feel? How did you react? How did they react?

▌ The coach's job is not to solve the problem

Types of questions

The following table highlights some of the most useful question types with some examples and suggestions for when you might use them. We also highlight some less useful types of questions that should be avoided when coaching or mentoring others.

TABLE 6.1 Useful questions and ones to avoid

Useful questions

Open questions

These are questions which elicit more than a one-word or yes/no answer. They encourage the coachee to elaborate on and explore issues. They can be categorised into several different types, each with their own purpose and use.

Type of question	When to use	Example
Searching questions	When you want to encourage the coachee to explore and expand on a topic.	'What would you be willing to change to achieve your goal?' 'What would you be unwilling to let go of?'
Clarifying questions	When you want to make sure you have fully understood the situation or the coachee's meaning. When you want to clarify what the coachee is saying.	'If I understand you correctly you are suggesting . . .' 'What, specifically, does that look like?'
Creative questions	When you want to stimulate the coachee's thinking, encourage new ideas or to prompt them to reflect a little more about an issue.	'What would you do if there were no barriers?' 'Let's get creative, what about some new ideas for solving this?'
Process questions	To help the coachee to reflect about their needs and actions in the coaching process. To help the coachee to focus on their objectives. They are essential during the contracting phase.	'What would you like to get out of this coaching session?' 'How do you think I can help you?'

→

Type of question	When to use	Example
Follow up questions	To get more information and understand the coachee's rationale and motivations.	'How do you think you would do that?' 'How will this action contribute to your goal?'
Reflective questions	To reflect back to the coachee part of their statement to encourage them to reflect more deeply about a particular issue or situation. To help uncover emotions and feelings.	'You say he was unhappy . . . how did he show his unhappiness?' 'You said you were feeling very emotional about the situation . . . what in particular were you feeling?'
Questions to avoid		
Leading questions	A question that presupposes the answer.	'We are in agreement on that, aren't we?' 'You find her quite challenging as well, don't you?'
Closed questions	Questions that elicit a one-word or yes/no answer. Questions that close conversation down.	'Have you done anything about it?' 'Do you agree?'
Multiple questions	Asking several questions at the same time.	'How do you feel about this situation now?' 'Are you upset or happy about the outcome?' 'What do you think your next steps should be?'

Here are some examples of good coaching questions:

▌ What have you already tried?

▌ Imagine this problem has already been solved. What would you see, hear, feel?

▊ What's standing in the way of an ideal outcome?

▊ What's your own responsibility for what's been happening?

▊ What early signs are there that things might be getting better?

▊ Imagine you are at your most resourceful. What do you say to yourself about this issue?

▊ What are the options for action here? So, what's the next/ first step?

▊ How does that feel?

▊ Say more . . .?

▊ Can I check that I have really understood the points that you are making here? What you feel/think is . . .

▊ So, to summarize so far . . .

▊ What have you tried so far?

▊ What happened?

▊ Tell me more . . .

▊ So . . .? (if you use this to prompt it must be used in conjunction with an enquiring voice and facial expression to match)

▊ Can you give me an example?

▊ Anything else?

▊ What else? And keep repeating, What else?

Don't start a coaching conversation by asking, *'What's the problem?'* This is a very common mistake especially if the coachee hasn't actually mentioned the word problem. It will make the coachee defensive, and could make them ask *'Do you see it as a problem?'* It is much better to ask, *'What's on your mind?'* or *'What's the issue?'* These are far less loaded.

Good-quality inquiry is the essence of coaching. Developing your skill in this area is vital. As a manager or leader you can work on this in many of your day-to-day interactions, not just when you are coaching. Get into the habit of asking questions and inquiring before advocating or telling. Quite apart from helping in developing as a coach this practice will also contribute to your leadership ability.

> Good-quality inquiry is the essence of coaching

Tips for success

▌ Questioning and inquiring allows your coachee to discover more for themselves.

▌ Allow time for your coachee to respond to any questions: a good question encourages reflection and will require thought before response.

▌ Ask more then you tell or advocate.

▌ When coaching, use mainly open questions.

▌ Develop your skill by practising questioning in everyday interactions.

7

Observing body language and non-verbal behaviour

As a coach you must be aware of both the impact of your own body language and non-verbal behaviour and be conscious of your coachee's behaviour.

Regarding your own behaviour, building a good-quality coaching relationship will require you to be consistent in your behaviour, words and actions towards others, not only during coaching sessions but at all times. As a coach your coachees will notice not only what you are saying but how you say it and what you are doing while you are communicating with them. The quality of your relationship, particularly concerning developing rapport, trust and mutual respect, will be defined by both the words and more importantly your non-verbal behaviour and body language.

> Be consistent in your behaviour, words and actions towards others

Your powers of observation are very important when coaching. Being aware of nuances in the coachee's language, non-verbal communication and body language will enable you to have greater understanding of their challenges, issues and feelings and to develop a meaningful coaching relationship.

The channels of communication

When you are involved in a coaching relationship you communicate via words (what you actually say), paralinguistics (how you say your words) and body language (what you do while talking and listening to others). In order to be truly effective as a coach you must understand the impact made and impression created by the way you communicate. In addition to this you must observe the way your coachee communicates with you and learn to read both the explicit and implicit messages being conveyed.

> You must understand the impact made and impression created by the way you communicate

So, for instance, your coachee may be telling you about a challenging relationship with a colleague and saying that, *'it's going ok'*, but what you pick up from the way they are expressing their message both verbally (the words are not said with enthusiasm nor is there any indicator of why it's going well) and via body language (eye contact may not be held, and facial expression may indicate lack of belief) is that all may not be so well. The effective coach will pick this up and explore it. Of course, this has to be done in an empathetic way so that the coachee can share with you as much or as little as they wish. So you might say something like: *'I am sensing that you want to explore this a bit more, so tell me more: what in particular is going well and what do you think you would like to continue to work on to improve things further?'* By probing a bit further you have responded to your instincts that all is not well, yet you have not directly mentioned that the coachee's words and non-verbals are incongruent.

So, as a coach what do you have to be aware of? You need to understand and manage your own communication channels and be able to read those of others. One of the early pioneers in the area of body language and non-verbal communications was Professor Albert Mehrabian, who explored the communication of our feelings and attitudes and the impact of the various channels of communication used. This information is of particular use to coaches and mentors. Typically, during any coaching or mentoring discussion you will be exploring feelings, emotions and attitudes. So what did he find?

He suggests that when communicating with others about your feelings, attitudes or emotions it is likely that only 7 per cent of the message is conveyed in the words, 38 per cent is conveyed by way of your paralanguage and 55 per cent is conveyed via your body language. (Be aware that this model is frequently misrepresented and these statistics only relate to communications relating to emotional intent.) There will be occasions when words have more importance than body language, for instance if you are sharing the annual results of your business, people will be listening for

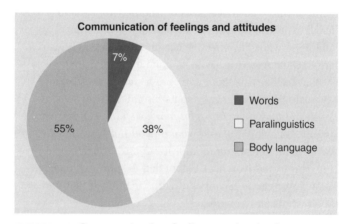

FIGURE 7.1 Communicating feelings and attitudes

Source: adapted from Mehrabian, A., *Silent Messages: Implied communication of emotions and attitudes* (Wadsworth Publishing Company, 1972)

the data rather than watching your body language. What do these statistics mean for you the coach? Quite simply it suggests that we get most of our cues and clues about a person's emotional intent from their non-verbal behaviour rather than from the words they use. As a coach you must therefore be tuned into how people express their emotions.

> As a coach you must therefore be tuned into how people express their emotions

This does not mean that you can ignore the words people say; we are simply suggesting that where feelings, attitudes and emotions are concerned you must focus more on non-verbal elements of the communication. Let's look at each of the three areas:

- **Words** convey our thoughts and ideas to others. The words we use and the way we construct the message are important in order to avoid misunderstanding and confusion. Words have real power, and it is important to think clearly about the words you use when coaching. Pay attention to the effect your language has on your coachee and be aware of the typical words and language used by them, so that you can pick up any nuances that could indicate changes in mood or emotion.

- **Paralinguistics** refers to the way you use your voice – your tone, pace, emphasis, volume, enunciation and silences. A change in the way a person is using their voice is one of the most powerful indicators of a change in feelings, emotion and attitude. The type of indicators you should be on the lookout for are:

  – **Variations in tone** can be a sign of changes in a person's feelings. For instance, a raised intonation can mean a person is querying an issue, or showing surprise or shock, while a decrease in tone can mean disinterest or anxiety.

— **Changes in the pace of speech.** For instance, if a person suddenly speeds up, this might indicate delight, distress or anger. While a slow pace suggests a person is expressing concern or thinking deeply before talking.

— **Emphasis on certain words** can highlight where an issue is focused. For instance, I *really* don't care! (Where the emphasis is on the *really*) might indicate the exact opposite.

— **The volume of a person's voice** can indicate several things. A loud voice might indicate anger, excitement or frustration; while a soft, low voice might suggest shyness or uncertainty.

— **Good enunciation**, where an issue is expressed clearly and concisely, would indicate confidence and knowledge. Poor enunciation, where the issue is expressed with a lack of clarity, will suggest uncertainty and lack of confidence. It would also make it hard for someone to understand the message.

— **Pausing and silence** is often a feature of a person's way of expressing themselves. What you need to watch out for here are changes in the patterns of pauses and silences that can indicate changes in emotion.

▌**Body Language** is a major aspect of the way we communicate and can unintentionally reveal many cues and clues as to how a person is feeling. Our physical behaviour in relation to our facial expression, gestures, posture, eye contact and proximity all contribute to the impression we are having upon another person.

Awareness of your own body language is vital as you must be aware of the messages that are seeping through to your coachee from the way you behave. Being natural is important. You should be your natural self and at the same time be aware of the impact of your body language on the other person.

As far as your coachee is concerned you must diligently observe their body language and in particular be aware of changes in typical patterns that might indicate changes in feelings, attitudes or emotions. It is these changes that signal when it might be appropriate to question, probe or explore the issue in more depth. When you do notice a change you may prompt them by saying something like, *'You look concerned?'* or *'You look a bit puzzled'*.

Let's look at some of the main areas to be aware of:

— **Facial expression** is the movement of our eyebrows, nose, forehead and mouth that leads to changes in the way our face is perceived. Slight changes in eyebrow movement, for instance raising the eyebrow, can indicate a change in mood towards or reaction to something.

— **Gestures** are the movements made by our hands, arms, fingers, legs and head. Again, a change in someone's normal pattern of behaviour is what you are on the lookout for when coaching. For instance, someone who normally sits very still with minimal gesturing who suddenly becomes very animated might indicate a change in feeling, attitude or emotion about the topic under discussion.

— **Posture** is about how people physically carry themselves. How you orient yourself towards others, sit, stand and move about are all indicators of how we are feeling. The way you position yourself during a coaching session is important, so be aware how you both sit as this can help get a session off to a good start. Sit upright in the chair, arms loosely in your lap and legs crossed in front of you – this is a fairly neutral posture that will enable you to develop your posture and body language in general as the meeting progresses.

— **Eye contact** is one of the most important aspects of body language; it is often referred to as gaze level. It has been found by researchers that people who make and hold higher levels of eye contact will tend to be regarded as trustworthy, confident, assertive, capable and sincere. While those with low levels of eye contact are often regarded with suspicion, thought of as shy and retiring, and on occasions rude. However, it is important to be aware of the cultural context here. In some cultures it is considered impolite to look directly at someone for long periods. This is the case in some Asian and Middle Eastern countries and as a general rule you may find that women in these cultures avoid direct gaze with men.

– **Proximity** was first explored by Edward Hall in the 1960s when he categorised proximity into four distinct areas:
  - Intimate – quite close, usually up to 18 inches and indicates closeness and intimacy
  - Personal – usually between 2 to 4 feet and is often a feature of the way people behave with close friends and family
  - Social – typically between 4 and 10 feet and used when interacting in social settings with people who are business colleagues or acquaintances
  - Public – anything more than 10 feet often used when speaking in public or in large groups

Changes in proximity and some sort of physical contact may indicate the level of comfort between two people. Closeness indicates comfort while distance will not necessarily indicate discomfort but rather lack of intimacy. Again cultural preferences will have an impact here.

The most important thing is to be aware of your own and the other person's usual way of expressing themselves. Coaching is always a two-way process and your coachee will notice any changes in how you are expressing yourself just as easily as you notice their changes. It is important to listen and observe your coachee, but also to be aware of your own emotional reactions. If you perceive changes in your coachee's behaviour during your sessions this is a sign that it might be worth probing around the issue being discussed.

Changes in your own behaviour are also worth noticing and reviewing after the session to help you understand your own coaching behaviour. During any conversation our vocal usage and body language will vary; the important issue is to be aware of any significant changes that affect the flow and sense of the session.

Be aware of your own emotional reactions

Tips for success

- Focus on both your own non-verbal behaviour and observe your coachee's.

- Be aware of your own non-verbal habits.

- Get into the habit of noticing peoples' non-verbal behaviour in everyday interactions.

- Ask your coachee and others for feedback about the impact of your non-verbal behaviour.

- Remember, body language involves what you do while you are talking and listening, as well as how you say things.

- What you say is important, but what you do while talking and how you say things is even more important for building rapport, trust and quality relationships.

- If you notice changes in your coachee's non-verbal behaviour point it out to them and inquire about it.

Building rapport and trust

Successful coaching relationships require a bond of trust and respect, and in our experience successful line managers will work hard at establishing these. The starting point for this is when rapport is being developed. Some people have a natural talent for rapport building, they seem to develop relationships and make connections with great ease. While this may come naturally to some, most people have to develop and work at this skill.

> Successful coaching relationships require a bond of trust and respect

Rapport is the process of making connections and building relationships with others and if effective will lead to feelings of mutual trust and respect between those people. Building genuine rapport involves subtlety and patience and can't be rushed. Rapport, trust and respect are essential for good-quality and long-term coaching relationships.

How to build and develop rapport

Here are some simple things you can do to help you in this area.

▌ Be aware of first impressions. Getting off to a good start in any relationship is essential, and as a coach you should be very aware of the impression you are creating, or the impression the coachee may already have of you if they are a direct report. So think about how you will greet your coachee:

– Facial expression – a relaxed smile while establishing eye contact with your coachee is a good start.

– Make sure your appearance and the environment where you are meeting is appropriate for the session.

– After the initial greetings quickly ask an open question to get the coachee talking – so, if you are meeting the person for the first time you could ask, *'Tell me a bit about yourself'*, or *'Tell me about your job and your organisation.'* Alternatively, if you already know the person, *'Tell me a bit about what's happened with you since last we met.'* Or, if they are a direct report ask, *'Tell me what your thoughts are about . . .?'*

– Think about how you will introduce yourself or the session. For instance, when meeting a new coachee for the first time we find the following process useful: introduce yourself, quickly ask them to talk about themselves – who they are, who they work for, their job, any personal information they want to share – and then ask for early thoughts about the coaching session. Only then will we move on to a brief introduction about ourselves. If we are coaching someone we already know, then chatting for a little time about something we have in common, or something we discussed at a previous meeting is a good starting point.

▌ Find common ground. Establishing something you have in common is a great way of developing rapport and liking for another person. Asking questions to find out about jobs, experience, hobbies, family life or whatever seems appropriate, will help you to find a common interest or experience. Finding this common ground gets you into conversation and sets the ball rolling for relationship development.

▌ **Demonstrate empathy**. Show others that you have emotional awareness. Empathy is about recognising and understanding another person's perspective and emotional state, and being able to react accordingly. Typically it will involve being attentive and focusing on the other person, listening and observing to be sure you are on the other person's wavelength and reacting and responding appropriately.

> ▌ Empathy is about recognising and understanding another person's perspective and emotional state

▌ **Use mirroring.** This is where you demonstrate empathy – adjusting your behaviour by reflecting the other person's body language, vocal usage and language. Care must be taken when mirroring as it is NOT simply copying the other person. Typically it will involve listening to and observing the other person and then responding with a similar vocal style in terms of paralinguistics. You may also consider the language you use. You can choose to use simple direct language, emotional language, jargon or more technical language depending upon the other person's language usage. Mirroring the other person's body language is also part of the process; so, for instance, if they are sitting in a relaxed manner then you should do this as well. Again, care must be taken not to mimic the other person; the purpose of mirroring is to make the other party feel comfortable and understood.

Once you get going and rapport seems to be established, then over time this will lead to a higher level of trust and respect. This of course does not happen overnight, and it will take time to fully build and develop to a naturally trusting relationship. So, having established rapport you must continue to develop the relationship to ensure you move further towards building a trusting and mutually respectful relationship.

Building trust

There are certain characteristics that seem to be present in any trusting and respectful relationship, as set out in Figure 8.1.

Let's look at each of these characteristics and explore in more detail what each actually involves and how you can demonstrate them in the context of the coaching relationship.

▌ **Dependability** is about fulfilling your promises and doing what you say you will do. So, for instance, if during a coaching discussion you say you will forward the coachee some information, or a follow-up email, make sure you do this, and in a timely manner. We tend to find that following up within 24 hours (assuming this is possible) is best. If you cannot provide the information always explain why to the coachee. Remember you want to develop trust so you must work on your dependability and reliability in doing what you say you will do.

▌ **Honesty** means ensuring you always tell the truth. For instance, if your coachee asks for feedback make sure you are straightforward and direct. So, if you are feeding back on

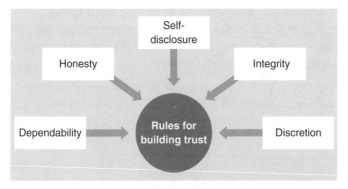

FIGURE 8.1 Characteristics for building trust

something that you believe the person could have done more effectively, be truthful and tell them, but in a positive way. You could try saying something like: '*I think you could have dealt with that situation in a more effective way. I know that you have done so in the past (then perhaps remind them of a time when they have) so let's reflect . . . How do you think you could have reached a better outcome?*'

▮ **Self-disclosure** demonstrates openness to giving information about yourself. You can disclose relevant and appropriate information that helps build the coaching relationship. For instance, if you are coaching someone about dealing with a challenging relationship you might share a piece of information demonstrating that on occasions you too have had challenges in some relationships. This should be done without giving away confidences and must be true. In using such self-disclosure you must of course ensure that you then go on to help the person work through their own situation and develop a plan to deal with it that suits the coachee.

▮ **Integrity** is about adhering to a set of principles such as consistency, fairness and professionalism in your relationship. As a coach you have many tools and techniques to draw on, many of which are covered in this book. Using these techniques and demonstrating your competence will help build trust and respect. Professionalism as a coach can be demonstrated by your ongoing professional development. For instance, working with a supervisor (see Chapter 27) or being part of a coaching action learning network.

▮ **Discretion** is critical for any coach. A lack of discretion more than anything will ruin a relationship. Especially if you are a line manager who is adopting a coaching approach. Any information imparted to you by any coachee must never be repeated except between you and the coachee.

Building rapport, trust and respect take time, patience and commitment – and yet it can take seconds for trust to be broken. Some of these reasons include: being caught out telling a lie; breaking a confidence; being caught out gossiping; and not delivering on promises.

> **It can take seconds for trust to be broken**

As Stephen R. Covey said:

> Trust is the glue of life. It's the most essential ingredient in effective communication. It's the foundational principle that holds all relationships.

Tips for success

▌ Never take trust for granted.

▌ Trust might be intangible but if you don't build it then your coaching will not be effective. Lack of trust in a coaching relationship has tangible consequences.

▌ Trust develops over time – it is all about developing rapport, respect and quality relationships.

▌ Focus on the impression you are making on others during any interaction.

▌ To build rapport, find common ground and demonstrate empathy.

▌ It can take a long time to build trust yet it can disappear in seconds, so:

  – Be dependable

  – Be honest

  – Use self-disclosure and openness

  – Demonstrate integrity in all you do

  – Be discrete – confidentiality is key

Challenge

Having the ability to challenge others in a professional yet empathetic way is a difficult skill to master. It is very easy for a challenge to sound like disapproval and to be perceived negatively. It is a good idea to talk about challenge as part of the contracting phase so that your coachee is forewarned about this aspect of your coaching approach. A good challenge will tend to move your coachee out of their comfort zone and help them explore assumptions, raise awareness and develop new ideas. The skill is not to make your coachee feel intimidated or vulnerable.

> A good challenge will tend to move your coachee out of their comfort zone

Why challenge is important

The purpose of challenge is to force the coachee to go beyond any self-imposed limits. As a coach your role is not to give advice and solutions to your coachee, but rather to explore their issues with them, and help them discover their own solutions.

Although you can't usually give advice, what you can do as well as supporting and encouraging the coachee is to challenge their thinking and assumptions. It's quite difficult to do both as most of us have a preference for one or other of these, but mastering the balance between support and challenge is one of the critical roles of the coach. Writer David Firth in his book *The Corporate Fool* (1998) tells us that if organisations are to survive they need to develop two core competencies: first, seeing things as they really are, and second, coming up with innovative solutions. The point of coaching is to ensure that employees do both of these. Your job as a coach is to support the coachee to help them develop new ways of thinking and behaving and challenge them to see things as they really are and as they could be.

If there is no challenge at all from the coach then the coachee can remain complacent and in denial about some of the issues they are facing. But this challenge needs to be done in a positive and sophisticated way. Crude and unskilful challenge would only lead to defensiveness by the coachee. It can be difficult to know how and when to challenge the coachee, and if you are not used to challenging in the coaching context, you can easily fall back on either not challenging at all, or over-challenging. So add challenge to your toolkit as one of your key coaching skills.

> Add challenge to your toolkit as one of your key coaching skills

How to challenge

Challenge requires you to consider both timing and balance. Timing in the sense that you pave the way to ensure your coachee is in the right frame of mind. For instance, sometimes coachees have to let off steam and if you jump in too early during this phase you will block the emotional release and your challenge will fall on deaf ears. Balance is needed because it is important to make sure you neither over-challenge nor under-challenge.

Coaches can often fall into the trap of over-challenging. This means a clumsy challenge that only leads to the coachee either closing down and saying nothing, or becoming defensive. There are obviously clumsy challenges like saying, *'That's a rubbish idea.'* Which of course would be unhelpful. But what is less obvious is when you say something like, *'Do you think that's a good idea?'* At first glance this might appear to be quite a reasonable challenge, but it has only two possible answers. Either the coachee says no it's not, or yes it is. The first option is unlikely as the coachee has just put the idea forward so it would be strange if they suddenly changed their mind! So the challenge is not really useful. The second option is more likely – the coachee having just proposed the idea clearly thinks it's a good one (even if you don't). So as a coach you are left with nowhere to go, unless you fall into the trap of then giving the coachee your own opinion that you don't actually think their idea is good. But now you are not coaching any more, just giving your coachee the benefit of your personal perspective.

> Coaches can often fall into the trap of over-challenging

So how can you make it more sophisticated? You can make it more open by asking something like, *'Can you explain to me how you would see that working?'* This challenge doesn't limit the coachee to a yes or no answer, but forces them to reflect more deeply on their idea, without any judgement by the coach. Another way of challenging skilfully is just to signal or flag your intent to challenge by saying something like, *'Can I just challenge your thinking here?'* followed by the challenge which might be, *'How sure are you about this?'*, or *'What assumptions are you making?'* Signalling or flagging has the effect of forewarning your coachee that a challenge is coming and therefore softening the effect.

Something that you do need to challenge is when your coachee uses words like 'always' or 'never', as in, *'She's **always** criticising me'*, or, *'He **never** praises me'*. In general there is rarely an instance of something always or never happening, so it is your job to politely inquire and ask, for example, *'Always? Do you mean that every time she sees you or talks to you she criticises you?'*

Similarly people often say things like, *'Nobody helps me!'* Again you need to challenge the word 'nobody'. A variation that we often hear is, *'Nobody ever helps me!'* And then you can say, *'Nobody . . .? Ever . . .?'*

Something else to look out for is the use of self-limiting words such as, 'can't' and 'couldn't', as in, *'I can't do that'*, or, *'I could never do that'*. Again, it is rare that the coachee really cannot do the thing they are talking about. It's more a case of they don't think or believe they can do it. So your job as a coach is to explore with the coachee why they think they can't do something, and help them understand where their fears and self-limiting beliefs come from. Then identify what they can do about reducing these beliefs and start to think about what they *can* actually do.

Tips for success

▮ Discuss challenge as a critical aspect of your coaching relationship so that your coachee expects some tough questions.

▮ A good-quality challenge will help your coachee to develop new ideas.

▮ Make sure your coachee is in the right frame of mind to be challenged.

▮ Formulate your challenge to encourage your coachee to think beyond their comfort zone.

▮ Don't challenge just for the sake of it.

▮ Don't over-challenge – balance is important.

10
Reflective skills

Developing skills to encourage reflection in others is useful for a coach or mentor. Reflection is a dynamic process, which enables you and your coachees to move forward and develop new ideas about, and understanding of, a situation. Reflection is a way of getting people to think or reflect about the way they did something or the way they experienced something. When you use your reflective process skills your coachee will be encouraged to evaluate these situations in a variety of ways, challenging their assumptions and experiences so that they can truly understand and bring new ideas and knowledge to any situation. Reflecting allows the coachee to 'hear' themselves as others perceive them.

> Reflecting allows the coachee to 'hear' themselves as others perceive them

For instance, when coaching a colleague about a job issue, you might notice changes in their body language and non-verbal behaviour which prompts you to reflect back in the following way: *'I notice that when you spoke about client management you sat up straighter, your face looked more animated and you spoke more enthusiastically – why might that be?'* This promotes further exploration and discussion about the issue. A good coach will enable the coachee to reflect about both the event and situation itself, and their feelings and emotions. Once your coachee has the ability to effectively reflect they will gain greater insight into many events and situations they face.

Skills for reflection

To encourage reflection there are a set of particular skills you need to be aware of, these include:

▌ **Patience** is vital for developing an effective coaching relationship and in order to encourage reflection which can often be quite time-consuming. As a coach you may sometimes feel the urge to offer ideas or give advice, but, as we already know, coaching is so much more effective if the coachee reaches their own conclusions and develops their own plan of action. So when you are encouraging someone to reflect and delve deeper into an issue, demonstrate patience and resist the temptation to offer advice, guidance or ideas. Usually good-quality reflection aided by some of the following skills will lead the coachee to their own outcomes. When they get to the outcome by themselves they are much more likely to be committed to the action and its implementation.

> Demonstrate patience and resist the temptation to offer advice, guidance or ideas

▌ **Curiosity** is essential for good reflection and you must be truly interested in helping your coachee to fully understand, explore and expand on the issue for themselves. You will help them to broaden out their thinking by examining their issue from multiple perspectives so that they can reach their own conclusions. Curiosity is demonstrated by your ability and energy to inquire and ask wide-ranging questions, and by showing genuine interest in the coachee and their situation. (See Chapter 6 on questioning.)

▌ **Testing understanding** demonstrates evidence of good listening. It involves reflecting words and feelings back to the coachee so that you can determine whether or not you have understood them. This in turn can make the coachee think further about the issue to encourage a broader understanding of both the situation itself and their feelings about it. It is a form of paraphrasing where you, the coach, restate what you have heard from the coachee.

For example, if your coachee has been talking about a problem with a couple of colleagues who he feels are ignoring him, you could simply say something like, *'So you think they are ignoring you?'* By repeating back the coachee's own words you will not only show that you have been listening but will also encourage them to continue reflecting about this. Of course you have to be careful not to overuse this type of short reflection, so another way of testing understanding is to paraphrase what you think you have heard in your own words. When paraphrasing you can reflect both the content of what they say and the feelings they are demonstrating. For instance, you could say, *'You are feeling frustrated about being disregarded by these colleagues?'* By reflecting both the content and feeling communicated to you, the coachee will be encouraged to explore further and develop a clearer focus about the situation or issue.

▌ **Clarifying** is a form of reflection that uses questions to determine that the coach fully understands what the coachee is saying. Clarification is often used when complex, confused or muddled messages are being conveyed. This is a particularly important skill when coaching or mentoring due to the often emotional nature of these discussions. When emotions run high people can become less clear and articulate in telling their story. If this is the case the coach may find it difficult to make sense of what their coachee is trying to articulate.

Clarification is helpful in two ways. First, it shows that you are listening with the aim of truly understanding what the coachee is getting at. Second, it reduces misunderstanding; a good clarifying question will get the coachee to respond by either agreeing, or by elaborating further. When using clarifying questions what you are interested in is judging the accuracy of your perception of the situation. The important aspect of clarification is that your questions must be non-judgemental, as your purpose is to establish meaning and understanding. So for instance useful clarification questions might be:

— Help me understand what you mean by giving me an example?

— I am not quite sure I understand your main point. Perhaps you could just recap what you said?

— When you said you were confused did you mean that you did not understand their point?

Good clarification will encourage your coachee to speak frankly, openly and honestly because it shows that you are actively listening, and are keen to completely understand the issue. The benefit to the coachee is that by you encouraging reflection through clarification, they then tend to expand their perspective and can examine the issue in more detail.

▍ **Summarising** is another important component of reflection. However, a summary should be used to recap what has taken place during a coaching session or part of a coaching session. For instance, you might say something like, '*Let me summarise where I think we are.*' The summary serves to draw together the various points discussed during the session in a succinct and straightforward way. Any summary is given from the coach's perspective. This is your opportunity to check out that you have understood the main elements of the session (or part of the session). The coachee can then add more information, or indeed correct any inaccuracies or misperceptions. When summarising, you must select the most important and essential points from your meeting and state them in your own words to ensure that you have fully understood. You may find that taking brief notes during your session will help you to summarise effectively. These notes will act as a memory jogger, but will also serve as a record of each meeting.

The following model, which is adapted from Davies (2012), might prove useful when thinking about how to incorporate reflection skills into your coaching practice:

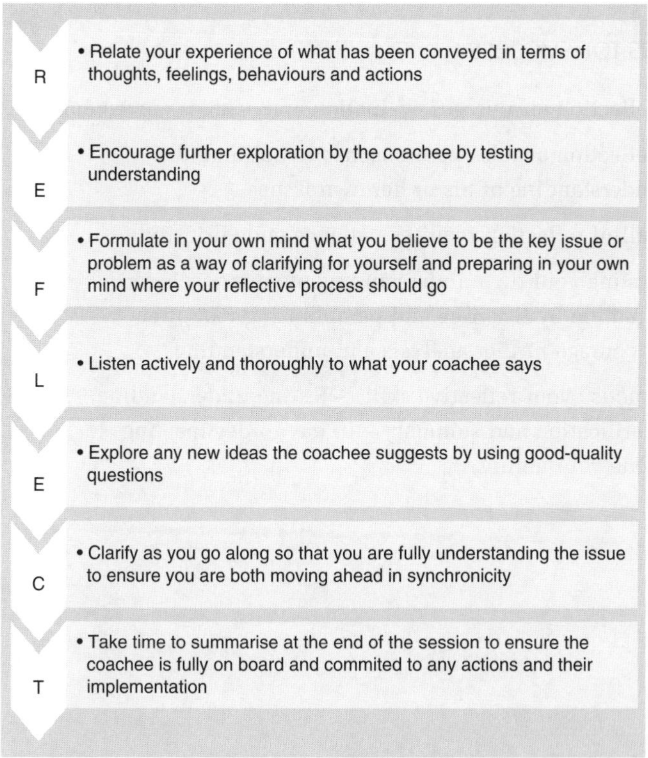

R
- Relate your experience of what has been conveyed in terms of thoughts, feelings, behaviours and actions

E
- Encourage further exploration by the coachee by testing understanding

F
- Formulate in your own mind what you believe to be the key issue or problem as a way of clarifying for yourself and preparing in your own mind where your reflective process should go

L
- Listen actively and thoroughly to what your coachee says

E
- Explore any new ideas the coachee suggests by using good-quality questions

C
- Clarify as you go along so that you are fully understanding the issue to ensure you are both moving ahead in synchronicity

T
- Take time to summarise at the end of the session to ensure the coachee is fully on board and commited to any actions and their implementation

FIGURE 10.1 The reflective practice model

Source: adapted from Davies, S., Embracing reflective practice, *Education for Primary Care* (Radcliffe Health, 2012)

Reflection is an essential communication skill that demonstrates good-quality listening and helps to build open, honest and mutually respectful coaching relationships. Done well it can truly bring about transformational coaching sessions by enabling the coachee to reach their own conclusions and outcomes.

As Dr Bob Nelson, American writer and management consultant, said:

> You get the best effort from others not by lighting the fire beneath them but by building the fire within them.

Tips for success

▌ Reflection encourages evaluation and enables movement.

▌ Reflection enables your coachee to build a full understanding of his or her own issues.

▌ Skilful reflection requires patience and curiosity.

▌ Testing your own understanding of your coachee's situation by listening and paraphrasing will often encourage further analysis and understanding.

▌ Practise your reflective skills – testing understanding, clarification and summary – in day-to-day meetings to hone your ability.

Reframing 11

There is nothing good or bad but thinking makes it so.

William Shakespeare

Another key skill for the coach is to be able to help the coachee reframe their perceptions and understanding of situations, especially when the coachee's existing interpretation of a situation is not helpful or is a barrier to progress.

What is reframing?

Reframing is essentially changing the way you perceive an event or issue, and by doing that you change the meaning of that event. When you change the meaning, responses and behaviour to that event will also change. So sometimes it's really helpful to change the meaning so that the response is more relevant and more positive; in short, more effective. Reframing is deliberately looking at a situation from a different perspective and through a different lens, in order to help the coachee have a more useful and helpful frame or perspective on an issue.

> Reframing is essentially changing the way you perceive an event or issue

Reframing is extremely common in the world of selling and advertising. For instance, the vegetables kale and beetroot have always been regarded as slightly boring, but have recently been reframed as 'super foods' leading to a boost in their sales. Another example of a reframe comes from the inventor Thomas Edison when he said: 'If I find 10,000 ways something won't work, I haven't failed. I am not discouraged because every wrong attempt discarded is another step forward.' Basically he is reframing failure as a learning experience.

We always put a frame around a situation. Sometimes that frame is useful and other times it is unhelpful. We need to recognise what frame the coachee is using and if it's not helpful, learn how to challenge their existing frame and help them find other, more useful frames. A simple example would be during a game of golf where a golfer hits a shot into the bunker. If you are a golfer you'll know that some golfers react with fury, shout and curse, hit the ground with their clubs and generally beat themselves up. Other golfers, however, react calmly, tell themselves it's part of the game, and see it as an interesting challenge and an opportunity to learn a key part of the game – that is, how to get out of the bunker. Which frame is the most useful?

How to use reframing as a coach

Often the coachee will be using frames which are not all helpful and it is your job to try and offer the coachee other frames which are just as valid, but are actually less negative and more positive, more useful and more helpful. Take a look at the example below that illustrates a reframe.

Mike was working with a fitness coach and lifting some weights. Pleased that he was actually able to lift the weights the required number of times, Mike was quickly brought down to earth by his trainer who immediately said, *'These weights are too light!'* Now they hadn't felt at all light to Mike, so now he felt bad and discouraged and felt that his trainer was being dismissive. He thought he was doing well, but now realised that in the trainer's eyes he wasn't.

What could the trainer have said differently? Well he could have reframed his thought and made it more positive and less dismissive. He could have said, for example, *'I think you can do more . . .'*, which is positive and encouraging. Or something like, *'Mike, you are strong enough to lift a heavier weight!'*

> **It is your job to try and offer the coachee other frames which are just as valid**

Both of these are reframes of the original thought, but instead of being perceived negatively, they would be more likely to be perceived positively and offer encouragement to the coachee.

Another example of an unhelpful frame would be when you are coaching someone for their career development and they say, *'I've been so unsuccessful, I always seem to get to the final interview round and then don't get the job.'* This negative frame can lead to discouragement, lack of energy and commitment to the promotion they are seeking. To help them reframe the situation to a more positive perspective you would ask them a range of questions:

▍ How many jobs have you applied for? If they say four you can reframe by indicating that they have in fact made the final cut 75 per cent of the time, which is an excellent ratio.

▮ How many applicants were there for these jobs? If they
  say, for example, over a hundred, you can reframe by
  indicating that getting to the final round puts you in the
  top percentile of all applicants.

▮ What have you learned from these three experiences that
  will help you for the next time?

Questions such as these are all designed to encourage your
coachee to reframe their negative attitude to a more positive
and helpful one.

So, constantly be on the lookout for any unhelpful frames
that the coachee is using and try to help them reframe the
situation in a way that is more helpful. Be careful, of course,
to ensure that the reframes are realistic and meaningful to
the coachee.

▮ Encourage your coachee to reframe
their negative attitude to a more
positive and helpful one

Tips for success

▮ Reframing enables you to encourage your coachee to
  look at things from a different perspective – and thus
  sometimes change their thinking about that situation.

▮ Get used to recognising the frames that your coachee is
  using – listen actively.

▮ Challenge and encourage reflection about any unhelpful
  frames.

▮ Help your coachee to formulate new, more useful frames to
  help them move on.

Supportive skills

12

As a coach your role is not to give advice and solutions to your coachee, but rather to explore their issues with them, and help them discover their own solutions.

Although you should not usually give advice, what you can do instead is to support and encourage the coachee and also challenge their thinking and assumptions. It is quite difficult to do both as most of us have a preference for one or other of these, but mastering the balance between support and challenge is one of the critical roles of the coach. Your role as a coach is to support the coachee to help them develop new ways of thinking and behaving, and to challenge them to see things as they really are. We have discussed how to challenge in Chapter 9, so in this short chapter we will focus on supportive skills.

> Support the coachee to help them
> develop new ways of thinking and
> behaving

Why supporting is important

Supporting your coachee is critical. If all you were to do as a coach were to challenge, the coachee would soon become uncomfortable. Therefore what is needed is a skilful blend of challenging and supporting. Coachees are often worried or nervous and it is your job to notice what is going well and be supportive of any efforts the coachee is making which are helping them move forward. Using an appropriate level of supporting behaviour will help build your coachee's confidence and self-belief to work through difficult issues and try out new ideas.

How to support

Blind and unthinking support is not useful. What you need to do is look for evidence of where the coachee has really made an effort, and praise the effort. It's no good saying things like *'Good job'*, or other generalities. You need to be specific and think of praising the effort that the coachee has put in. You don't need to praise the result itself, but more the effort that has been put in. Your general attitude should be supportive. It is difficult enough to be a coachee when you receive feedback which is not always easy to hear, and are trying to change attitudes and behaviours without having any support.

> What is needed is a skilful blend of challenging and supporting

The four A's of supporting

We think that there are four critical aspects of supporting:

- Attending
- Acknowledging
- Affirming
- Appreciating

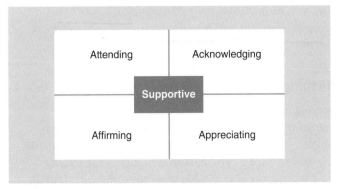

FIGURE 12.1 The four A's of supporting

Attending

It is important to show that you as a coach are fully present in the meeting. By 'fully present' we mean bringing all your senses, focus and awareness to the coaching session. You are not trying to play a role or be someone else, you just need to bring your authentic self to the session, and be prepared to let go of your own issues and concerns for the duration of the session. So then you can focus on the coachee, listen to them properly and show them that your attention is on them. This will lead to the coachee being able to fully share what's on their mind. If you are not prepared to focus fully on the session then it is unlikely that the coachee will either.

Acknowledging

One of the basic human needs is to be recognised and included. So it is important for you as a coach to be able to properly acknowledge what the coach is saying and also what he or she is feeling. This means showing patience and taking the coachee's issues seriously. We have noticed that some managers have a tendency to trivialise their coachee's concerns or issues during coaching sessions, by saying things like, *'Don't worry, you'll be fine!'* They may indeed be fine but it's not your job to say so – you don't actually know if they will be fine. Also the role of the coach is to listen to people's concerns and take them seriously, not to try somehow to make them appear less significant than they are.

Affirming

Affirming is building on the coachee's strengths – recognising them and reassuring the coachee about these strengths. It seems rather obvious to say this, but in practice many people have a very clear idea of their weaknesses, but a far less clear idea of what their strengths are. Effective performance comes from your strengths not from your weaknesses. As the late Insoo Kim Berg, co-founder of Solution Focused Brief Therapy, said: 'Always look at the person's resources first.' So, keeping an eye out for someone's strengths and resources, and then making sure you give the coachee feedback on them, is a key aspect to coaching.

Appreciating

This is about being positive and giving positive feedback to the coachee. So, as a coach you are aware of when the coachee has done something positive, or taken steps in the right direction. Then you share that with them. Research suggests that in general a ratio of three positive remarks or interventions to one critical one is helpful. Giving compliments is part of being appreciative; they are used to identify and highlight the coachee's strengths and resources, and any progress that has been made. It is very difficult for some managers to give compliments; it seems they would rather say nothing at all than say something positive to someone. It can, of course, be affected by culture. Some national and organisational cultures are masculine where giving praise and compliments can be viewed as a sign of weakness. There is a German proverb which says, 'Nicht geschimpft ist genug gelobt!', which in English means, 'Not criticising is sufficient praise!' You can imagine that giving praise and being appreciative in such cultures could be rather difficult. But we know from our research that many people, especially Gen Y, want a different style of leadership, one that is more coaching oriented and appreciative.

The first step to giving compliments and being appreciative is to be on the lookout for what people do well. Instead of doing what we usually do and being critical and judgemental, try noticing what you like, or what you value about something or someone. Suspend your judgement on the things you don't like for a moment and focus on the positive. Then share it in a straightforward and simple way, *'I like the way you did that.'* If you find that too difficult then try wrapping your compliment up in a question, for instance, *'How do you do that so effectively?'*

When you are next coaching someone try to suspend your critical self and remember the four A's – Attend, Acknowledge, Affirm and Appreciate.

> *Appreciation is a wonderful thing: it makes what is excellent in others belong to us as well.*
>
> Voltaire

Tips for success

▌ Show appreciation and support; this builds confidence and self-belief in others.

▌ When showing appreciation ensure you give evidence for that appreciation and that it is genuine.

▌ Suspend your natural critical self, look for the positives, then tell your coachee what you like.

▌ Pause before responding to your coachee and think about what they are feeling and how your responses might make them feel.

Feedback 13

When coaching you will often either be giving or receiving feedback. In this chapter we will discuss and explore giving and receiving feedback as part of the coaching and mentoring process. We will review some general guidelines for giving and receiving effective feedback and then move on to the specifics that are important to take account of in a coaching context.

Effective feedback

As a coach you will have to be skilled at providing feedback to your coachees and you should also be receptive to, and ask for, feedback from the people you are coaching. If you are taking part in coaching supervision (see Chapter 27) you may also receive feedback from the supervisor or others in the supervision group. Any feedback you either give or receive requires you to be sensitive, tactful and diplomatic. Here are some general rules that apply in any effective feedback situation:

> Any feedback you either give or receive requires you to be sensitive, tactful and diplomatic

▮ **Focus on behaviour you have experienced or observed, not on personality traits they cannot change.** The aim of behavioural feedback is to raise self-awareness of how the person's behaviour is perceived by you and how it might be perceived by others.

▮ **Be precise and detailed in your description of the behaviour.** Make sure it is not judgemental; it should simply be descriptive – even restating the coachee's own words if necessary. This is required to ensure the recipient has a good understanding of how you experienced their behaviour to encourage them to reflect about the impact it is having both on you and potentially others. For instance, rather than saying something like, '*You keep interrupting people*', be more specific and say something like, '*I noticed in the meeting this morning you interrupted Susan four times and each time she was not able to finish her point.*'

▮ **The feedback is owned by you.** It should therefore describe how it affects you. You must always remember that when giving feedback it is how **you** have perceived the individual and should not imply that others will have the same opinions, feelings or perspective. So always talk in the first person – use 'I' statements and try to avoid saying things like, '*People might think . . .*' or '*Others seem to . . .*'

▮ **Skilful feedback should be given at an appropriate moment.** This should be when you believe the recipient is at their most receptive. You should try to give any feedback about behaviour as quickly as possible after the behaviour has been experienced. However, coaching can sometimes involve emotional reactions to the issue being discussed – in such a situation you may have to time your feedback accordingly; you may, for instance, decide to leave your feedback until your next meeting.

▌ **Feedback should be constructive.** It should focus on encouraging reflection and improvement. You must always give careful consideration to what you are planning to say and how you will say it, ensuring your language and presentation is descriptive yet neutral and is non-evaluative and non-judgemental. So, for instance you could say something like: '*I like your focus on . . . and I'd like to hear how you think you could do even better?*'

▌ **Demonstrate sensitivity to the emotional impact of your feedback on your coachee.** We all have different responses to receiving feedback, so watch, listen and stop speaking. Give people time to assimilate, reflect about, respond to and deal with their emotional reactions to any feedback you give them. Be aware that you may have to elaborate on your initial feedback to help people understand. This may also mean that you have to modify your feedback or even stop giving feedback at that moment. Remember, it is supposed to be helpful to the coachee, not an opportunity for you to vent your feelings.

▌ **Be open to receiving feedback.** As a coach, manager or leader you should also be open to receiving feedback from others. This means that you should actively encourage and ask for feedback from your coachees and when it is given listen, test understanding and clarify to be sure you understand the feedback. Demonstrating that you are open to and actively learning from any feedback that you receive will have a positive effect on your credibility and reputation as a coach. It will also help towards building an open, trusting and respectful coaching relationship.

> You should also be open to receiving feedback from others

How people use any feedback they receive is, of course, up to them. All you can do is continue to observe their behaviour and perhaps offer feedback when you see any new behaviour being implemented – this reinforcement will help the coachee to recognise the importance of feedback for their development.

Coaching and feedback

As a coach you are in a privileged position in that you will be involved in working with coachees on issues that are challenging them in some way. This will often give you access to much more information about how people behave, think and work than other colleagues or their manager may have. Consequently this will lead to them sharing confidences, expressing themselves emotionally and generally disclosing information that they would not normally reveal to others. So, giving feedback under these circumstances can be a delicate affair. You may find that you have to be extremely observant and have all your emotional antennae on full alert in order to determine when feedback might be appropriate.

> Have all your emotional antennae on full alert

Feedback is one of the topics you should discuss during the early phases of the coaching relationship, during the 'contracting' and 'rapport building' phase. Both parties need to be clear about both giving and receiving feedback. So, for instance, you may agree with your coachee that you will offer feedback to them based on your reactions to and feelings about:

- Their behaviour towards you during the session.

- The behaviour they have described in relation to what they did in any situation or issue they have been working on with you.

▌ Ideas they are sharing with you about how they might deal
with situations in the future.

You may also suggest that it would be good to receive
feedback from them about how they are receiving you
as a coach. This could be a regular part of your session
where towards the end of each session you ask them for
feedback. The important thing is to set it up beforehand as
part of the process so that neither party is caught unaware.
Good-quality feedback requires a lot of thought, so prior
warning that it will be part of your session is beneficial. One
easy way of getting the process off to a good start is to frame
the feedback you would like. For instance, towards the end
of the first session you could ask the coachee to *'Share with
me one thing I did that you feel was of benefit'*, and likewise
to *'Share with me one thing I could do that would make
the session even more useful.'* These are useful questions to
make people feel more comfortable giving feedback.

You should also be aware that in any coaching meeting
people will 'let off steam' and during these times their
behaviour may be out of character. As this sort of behaviour
is probably not indicative of the way they normally behave
it is perhaps not fitting to give feedback about it. Allow them
to vent their emotions and then move on to discussing the
issues.

If, however, the behaviour is testing boundaries or trying
out ideas that are new ways of dealing with the challenges,
then these are the opportunities you are looking for.
Feedback from you about your reactions to, and feelings
about, how a piece of behaviour affected you may just help
the coachee to determine a future course of action or ideas
they may try out.

We all need people who will give us feedback. That's how we improve.

Bill Gates

Tips for success

▍ Be prepared to both give and receive feedback.

▍ Feedback requires you to use diplomacy and tact.

▍ Focus your feedback on behaviour you observe or experience and be constructive.

▍ Be detailed and precise when giving feedback.

▍ Use 'I' statements – own the feedback.

▍ Be aware of the emotional impact of your feedback.

▍ Actively encourage feedback from your coachees.

3 Part

Coaching approaches, models and tools

In this part of the book we will explore some of the most popular contemporary coaching approaches, models and tools. Many of these overlap one another and some of the key features and skills are very similar. The important thing for you as a leader or manager who wishes to build coaching into your day-to-day work is to understand the various approaches, models and tools. You can select those you wish to use during your coaching sessions. This is not an exhaustive list; it is, however, a list of the ones we feel to be most useful.

The approaches, models and tools shown here are all useful. We find that, with experience, people are able to draw on many of these. We also hear from managers that they create their own models and tools that then help them to structure and focus their sessions to suit their own style, situation and approach.

Coaching approaches

*A person cannot teach another person directly; a
person can only facilitate another's learning.*

Carl Rogers, psychologist

In this chapter we will introduce you to three of
the most popular contemporary coaching
approaches:

▊ Person-centred coaching

▊ Appreciative practice

▊ Solution-focused coaching

You will find that these approaches have some
commonalities and most of them have been developed based
on some of the fundamental principles of coaching that we
discussed in the early part of this book. You will often find
these concepts being referred to in coaching communities,
and as leaders, or managers as coaches, you should be aware
of the basic ideas and principles relating to each of them.
In each case we will offer references where you can explore
them more thoroughly.

Person-centred coaching

Person-centred coaching is largely attributed to Carl Rogers,
who described its theory and background in detail in his

book *Client-Centred Therapy* (1951). For the purposes of this book we will highlight some of the key aspects of person-centred coaching, which have been adapted from Rogers's original theory, as it applies to you the leader or manager as a coach in today's business world.

Rogers worked with five key assumptions when he developed his theories about person-centred learning:

▌ Individuals learn differently based on their own unique experience of the world.

▌ For learning to take place it must have relevance to the learner.

▌ Non-directive learning is most effective to gain commitment to change, and demands that the coach guides and encourages reflection rather than tells.

▌ People are more likely to learn in a trusting, open and friendly environment, and not when concepts and ideas are being forced upon them.

▌ During any learning session new ideas must be relevant to the individual and issue at hand to encourage open-mindedness and exploration of the new ideas.

Many current-day coaching, counselling, mentoring and psychotherapy practices have been developed based on Rogers's work. The main reason for this is that there is now much evidence to suggest that by using person-centred approaches you are more likely to lead the coachee to implementation of ideas and thus lasting change. So what does person-centred coaching mean for you, in practice?

First of all and most importantly, it is about focusing on the needs of the individual you are coaching – listening, questioning, observing and responding to their needs. By using these approaches you will encourage them to explore and work with you on the issue, and help them to develop their own plans, ideas and conclusions.

Your role will then be to use the five assumptions together with tools from your coaching toolkit to encourage the coachee to find their own solutions and to set realistic goals for change. Some of the tools you can use are explained in Chapter 16.

Person-centred coaching requires you to have patience, to be creative and to focus exclusively on the individual you are working with and their issue. This type of coaching requires you to be at your most flexible and have the ability to adapt, adjust and use approaches that will work for the coachee and their situation.

> Be at your most flexible and have the ability to adapt

Appreciative practice

> *Dreams are extremely important. You can't do it unless you can imagine it.*
>
> George Lukas

Another way of coaching is to look at what we can learn from appreciative practice. Appreciative practice owes its origins to work by David Cooperrider and his supervisor Suresh Srivastva, when he was studying for his PhD at Case Western Reserve University in the United States. David and his supervisor Suresh then went on to create the practice called 'appreciative inquiry' which is described in detail in Cooperrider's book *Appreciative Inquiry: A Positive Revolution in Change*. Using different forms of appreciative inquiry has become an increasingly popular approach in coaching and the term 'appreciative coaching' is now quite widely used.

We first encountered appreciative inquiry (AI) in 2000 where we also had the pleasure of meeting and working with Frank Barret, one of the co-founders of AI. Since appreciative coaching is based on the work of AI, it's worthwhile knowing a little bit more about it before we look at some of the things you can do in appreciative coaching.

There are a number of principles on which the concept of appreciative practice is based, and these are:

▌ **Inquiry is inseparable from action.** In other words asking good questions actually evokes change. So as a coach, rather than trying to solve someone's problem, you would choose to ask good questions and that by itself could make a big difference.

▌ **The stories we tell are important.** Our lives and organisations are full of stories and these affect the ways we think and act. So how we tell the story is critical, and by changing the stories we tell we can change the way we act. As a coach, you would pay particular attention to the stories the coachee tells and *how* they tell them. Is it helpful or unhelpful, are they in control or do they see themselves as a victim? Is the story positive or negative? If the stories are unhelpful or negative you can then help coachees tell different stories, or tell their story differently by helping them to frame and reframe their stories to be more useful and positive.

▌ **Positive images of the future lead to positive action.** By imagining and creating a positive vision of the future we can actually help create that future. So it is important to ask the coachee to imagine a better future and get them to actually create that better future in their mind. This is often done by asking the 'miracle' question, that is, where you ask the coachee to imagine they go to bed tonight and overnight a miracle happens and in the morning when they wake up, their problem has disappeared. You then ask the coachee what they are now experiencing with the problem gone. What are they doing? What are they seeing?

What are they saying? What are the other people involved doing? What are the other people saying, and so on.

Although this can be difficult for the coachee – many people automatically react by saying there is no such thing as a miracle – it is important to be persistent and ask them just to suspend their disbelief and try to create this new picture and scenario in their mind. In our coaching practice we have observed and experienced just how powerful the miracle question can be.

▌ **Positive questioning creates more long-lasting and effective change.** It is much more important to ask positive and appreciative questions than deficit-focused ones. Deficit-focused questions are ones like, '*What's the problem?*', '*Who's the weak link?*', '*What went wrong?*', '*Whose fault is it?*' Positive and appreciative questions will be ones like, '*What progress have you made?*', '*What has gone well?*', '*What do you do well?*', '*What are your strengths?*', '*When have you done that successfully before?*', '*How did you manage to cope so well?*'

The four D's of appreciative inquiry

Appreciative inquiry is used in many fields and often when dealing with change. There are four stages in AI, known as the four D's. The four D's are used to help participants create a different perspective of the change and then to work with others to co-create the change.

The four stages are:

▌ Discovery

▌ Dream

▌ Design

▌ Destiny

The four D's are used to help participants create a different perspective

When used in coaching, the **Discovery** stage would focus on finding out more about the issue, and the person's involvement, relationships and emotions around the issue. You would want to know what is going on, not to try to solve the issue but to help the coachee become more aware of, and clarify, their thoughts and feelings.

In the **Dream** phase you would want to explore potential and vision. What does the coachee want to achieve? What is their vision or their dream? What is their potential? What are their strengths and resources?

In the **Design** phase you would concentrate on creating actions, and look at specific actions and behaviours. What will the coachee do differently? How will they behave? What new practices and behaviours can they choose? How can they embed these different routines and behaviours? What small steps can they take that moves them in the desired direction?

In the **Destiny** phase you would look at how to maintain the changes and ensure that they are sustainable.

A nice way of summing up what appreciative inquiry is all about is given by Professor Gervase Bushe of Simon Fraser University in Canada. According to Professor Bushe: 'Appreciative Inquiry advocates collective inquiry into the best of what is, in order to imagine what could be, followed by collective design of a desired future state that is compelling and thus, does not require the use of incentives, coercion or persuasion for planned change to occur.'

Building on this definition and linking it to coaching practice you could build the following model of appreciative coaching:

- You would inquire not into the coachee's failings, but into their strengths and resources, perhaps helping them to integrate positive experiences and feedback they may already have.
- You would help them imagine a better future or desired state.
- You would then help them work through the design – that is, the actions and behaviours they need to put in place, in order to achieve the desired outcomes.
- You would ensure that you review how they are progressing in their goals and objectives.

To summarise, appreciative coaching is one more tool at your disposal to help you become a more effective coach. You probably won't use all the techniques, but you can borrow some of the methodologies described above in your everyday coaching.

Solution-focused coaching

The solution focus (SF) approach to coaching is an adaptation of a therapeutic model that came from the Milwaukee Institute of Solution Focused Brief Therapy where Steve de Shazer, Insoo Kim Berg and their colleagues practised what was then a radical approach to therapy. Paul Z. Jackson and Mark McKergow's book *Solutions Focus: Making Coaching and Change SIMPLE* gives a clear account of how you can use SF in business and coaching.

There are some basic assumptions and principles underlying the SF approach to coaching:

▊ The coachee has all the necessary resources to change.

▊ Change is happening all the time: the coach's job is to identify and amplify useful change. So the coach needs to inquire where useful change has already taken place.

> ## The coach's job is to identify and amplify useful change

▊ There is no one 'right' way of looking at things: different views may fit the facts just as well. The coach's role here is to challenge assumptions and perceptions.

▊ Detailed understanding of the 'problem' is usually little help in arriving at the solution. The coach does not have to spend huge amounts of time trying to understand the coachee's issue in great detail. Rather his or her job is to ask good open questions in order to help the coachee reflect on and become more aware of the issues.

▊ No 'problem' happens all the time. There are always times when the problem is NOT happening, so a useful way forward lies in identifying what is going on when the problem does not happen. Again the coach's role is to probe into when things are going well rather than when they are going badly. This can be unexpectedly difficult as coachees are often focused on the problem.

▊ Small changes in the right direction can be amplified to great effect. There seems to be a desire within organisations to effect big changes. But big changes are hard to achieve in reality. The SF approach stresses the importance of recognising and encouraging small steps that are going in the right direction.

▮ It is important to stay solution focused, not solution forced.

▮ It is useful to have the coachee imagine what a preferred future might look like. This takes the form of the so-called miracle question (in the same way as with AI) where the coach asks the coachee to imagine they have gone to bed and woken up the next day and a miracle has happened. Then the coach asks them to describe what is now happening. This is also quite a difficult technique, as often the coachee can resist the question and say that it is too difficult to answer, or become defensive and say that a miracle can't possibly happen! Nevertheless, it is worth persisting and getting the coachee to use their imagination and visualise their preferred future. Once they have done this it becomes more possible for the coachee to start describing the specific behaviours they will display in that future.

In the solution-focused approach it isn't necessary to delve into the roots of the problem or analyse the problem in detail. The focus, as its name suggests, is towards developing solutions, and in particular the coachee's own solutions. This is achieved through a variety of steps and processes which involve, first, finding the **Platform** – that is, what are we here to do today? Then you can move to **Counters**, which means asking about the coachee's strengths and resources. What do they have that will help them overcome their issue? Then you would ask **Scaling** questions – in other words where are they on a scale of 1 to 10, with 10 being high? If for example the coachee says they are a 3 then you can ask where they would like to be? What would it be like if they were at 5? What would they be doing? Saying? Feeling? Then you would move on to asking about what small steps could the coachee take in the right direction and then give some positive affirmations to the coachee, before perhaps asking them to try out a different way of doing things before your next session.

Problem-focused questions versus solution-focused questions

Imagine you are in a coaching situation and you were asking the following problem-focused questions. How do you think the coachee would react?

▌ What's wrong with what you're currently doing?

▌ Why are you doing so badly?

▌ What's the main reason for your difficulty?

▌ Whose fault is that?

▌ What other things make it so hard to improve?

▌ Why will it be difficult for you to get any better?

Compare that with the following solution-focused questions:

▌ What is it that you'd like to be better at?

▌ What are you aiming to achieve?

▌ How will you know you've achieved it?

▌ What was the best you have ever been at this?

▌ What went well on that occasion?

▌ What will be the first signs that you're getting better?

▌ How will other people notice this improvement?

These are much more positive, will give much more energy to the coachee and enable them to think positively about the strengths and resources they already have.

In summary, the SF approach focuses on exploring possible solutions rather than delving too deeply into the 'problem'. It tries to build on success and look at what works and then encourage people to do more of what works. It looks to discover skills and competencies that the coach already has, and which they might not even be aware of. And it stresses the importance of taking small steps in the right direction rather than huge leaps that might not actually happen.

Tips for success

▎ Using any of these coaching approaches will require practice.

▎ In any coaching session you may draw upon one or all of these approaches.

▎ Adapt and build on the approaches discussed to find your own natural approach and style – this is the most genuine.

▎ DO NOT slavishly follow rules – this will tend to come across as formulaic and will lessen your effectiveness as a coach.

Coaching models

I n this section we will introduce you to, and examine various processes and models that can be used during your coaching. The UK Chartered Institute of Personnel Development report in 2004 confirms that taking a structured rather than a random approach to coaching is more productive. If you are starting out on your coaching journey you will find that using a systematic and structured approach will help you focus, keep track and bring clarity.

All the models and processes shown here are useful and with experience you will be able to draw on all of them and eventually create your own processes and models. Some of the models are perhaps more useful than others and many of them seem to be acronyms – such as ACHIEVE, or PRACTICE or GROW, which might make them easier to remember, but may seem a little forced.

> A systematic and structured approach will help you focus, keep track and bring clarity

Key models and processes for coaching

We feel that it is important for you as a coach to be aware of the key coaching models that are regularly used. We present

FIGURE 15.1 Key models and processes for coaching

five of the most common and, in our opinion, most useful and relevant models. Having read them you might find that you have a preference for one of them. However, you may find that you prefer to develop your own unique model possibly based on some of the features of those discussed in this chapter. At the end of the chapter we will suggest how you might go about doing this.

ACHIEVE model

Let's start with the ACHIEVE model – created by Sabine Dembkowski and Fiona Elridge.

ACHIEVE stands for:

> **A**ssess current situation
> **C**reative brainstorming of alternatives
> **H**one goals
> **I**nitiate options
> **E**valuate options
> **V**alid action programme
> **E**ncourage design momentum

This is a good and useful model, which covers all the bases plus it is easy to remember.

▌ **Assess current situation** – ask open questions to help the coachee reflect on their current situation. What are they doing? What have they done? What are the implications of the situation? It is important to explore at this stage and not to give advice, ask leading questions or judge and evaluate.

▌ **Creative brainstorming of alternatives** – help the coachee to come up with other courses of actions. Keep probing and asking what else could you do? Again don't give any suggestions or advice.

▌ **Hone goals** – focus the coachee on specific goals as opposed to vague and general ideas about what they want. The more specific the goal the more likely it is that they can do something.

▌ Focus the coachee on specific goals as opposed to vague and general ideas

▌ **Initiate options** – help the coachee to develop options. It is important to ask the coachee to create new and different options from the ones they have already considered. It is also important to ask them to create several different options.

▌ **Evaluate options** – clearly the options have to be evaluated and the implications of these options considered from both a tactical and strategic perspective. The coach doesn't do the evaluation but rather asks the coachee good probing questions that help the coachee to think through the implications and choose the most feasible options.

▌ **Valid action programme** – this is where the coach helps the coachee reflect on what specific actions they will take. It is also important to ask what the level of commitment is.

▌ **Encourage design momentum** – in this stage you help the coachee ensure any actions they take are ongoing and sustainable.

PRACTICE Model

The next coaching model we'd like to look at is the
PRACTICE model. It was developed by Dr Stephen Palmer.
PRACTICE stands for:

>Problem identification
>Realistic relevant goals
>Alternative solutions generated
>Consideration of consequences
>Target most feasible solutions
>Implementation of . . .
>Chosen solutions
>Evaluation

This is an extremely effective and applied model that also
has the advantage of having an easily remembered acronym,
which, we must emphasise, is important when you are not
experienced or familiar with the coaching process. It gives
some more detail around the need to have realistic goals
and stresses the importance of using a solution-focused
approach. Let's take a look at the steps in more detail:

▎ **Problem identification** – clearly you need to start with the
issue, which by the way may not always be a problem.
What is the coachee's need? What help do they want?

▎ **Realistic relevant goals** – this is an extremely important
stage where you ask for the coachee's goals. And as Palmer
suggests, they need to be realistic and relevant to the issue.
You may find it quite difficult at times to actually tease
specific goals from the coachee, but you need to persist.
Otherwise at the end of the session you will realise that
you can't make any progress because you haven't managed
to get specific achievable goals from the coachee.

▎ **Alternative solutions generated** – this is a critical part of
the coaching process and is where you help the coachee to
generate different solutions or possibilities. The coachee
may have already tried various actions and your job here

is to ask them what they have already tried, how it went, and what could they do differently. This is actually quite a tough part of the coaching process as there may be a tendency by the coachee to ask you what your ideas are. Don't give your ideas here, just be patient and continue to ask what the coachee could do differently and help them to generate alternative solutions.

▌ **Consideration of consequences** – this step is where you invite the coachee to reflect on the implications and consequences of their ideal solution or options. Ask them to consider how people would react if they went ahead with their option. You can simply ask them, *'What would be the reaction if you did that?'*, *'How would the other person feel?'*, *'What would the implications be?'*

▌ **Target most feasible solutions** – based on the answers given to the question above, you can then help the coachee identify the options and solutions that are the most likely to be effective. By asking questions about the possible reactions to their ideas and options, you can help them filter out the ones that are likely to have negative consequences and help them towards the more effective ones.

▌ **Implementation of ... Chosen solutions** – we can group these two steps together as they really form one stage of the process. Here is where you focus on actual implementation of the solutions you have decided are most likely to be effective. So you can ask questions like, *'What will you do?'*, *'How specifically will you do it?'*, *'When will you do it?'*, *'Who will notice?'*, *'What will they notice?'*

▌ **Evaluation** – this final stage of the process is about reviewing any actions and evaluating the consequences of these actions. You will want to ask the coachee questions such as, *'What happened?'*, *'How did you feel it went?'*, *'What worked?'*, *'What didn't work?'*, *'What will you continue doing?'*, *'What will you do differently?'*, *'What will you keep on doing?'*

CLEAR model

Peter Hawkins created the CLEAR model and we like this model because, as its name suggests, it is clear and covers all the essential elements of a good coaching session.

CLEAR stands for:

Contract

Listen

Explore

Action

Review

■ **Contract** – an essential part of a coaching session is to ensure there is a clear contract with the coachee. What is the scope of the session? How much time do we have? What outcomes are wanted? What rules should we respect? What are the roles? What are the limits of a coaching intervention? It is also about being clear on issues like confidentiality and the scope of the session. In our experience we often find that managers skip this very important part of the coaching process and try to go directly to exploration of the issue.

> **Ensure there is a clear contract with the coachee**

■ **Listen** – this is where the coach listens actively. Ask open questions in order to help the coachee develop an understanding and awareness of their issue and take ownership. But the focus is more on listening attentively to the coachee with their eyes and intuition as well as their ears.

■ **Explore** – here the coach builds on the listening phase by asking probing questions, going deeper, and perhaps asking challenging questions. The coach will want to explore how the coachee's actions affect the situation, and help them become aware of their own assumptions, judgements and biases.

▌ **Action** – in this phase the coach focuses on what the next steps are. What will the coachee actually do? What will they do specifically? How will they do it?

▌ **Review** – this phase of the coaching conversation focuses on closing the session, summarising what was said and decided, asking questions about what was valuable, what was helpful to the coachee, what could be done differently? Here you also agree a time and place to review the actions which have been decided, and then of course follow up on what the coachee has been able to do, how it was received, and so on.

We have found the following two models particularly useful as practical frameworks for coaching. We don't recommend that you stick blindly to any one model, but they can be very useful when you are starting to use coaching in a more structured way.

GROW Model

Developed by Sir John Whitmore, the GROW model will be used by the coach to remember to find out the coachee's:

Goals
Realities
Options
Will

The idea is that the coach explores the coachee's specific goals and objectives, before then moving on to exploring what is going on in reality, what has been happening, what people have done and said, who is involved, and so on. Then the coach has the coachee develop a number of different options, before moving on to asking about the degree of will or commitment, and what energy the coachee has in order to take specific actions. It can appear a fairly obvious model, but it helps you to take a more structured coaching approach rather than just giving advice, so in practice it is very useful to have a model like this. In reality many managers start to coach without having fully explored the specific goals and then find themselves stuck.

We have created a modified version of this structure and added a couple more R's to the process. The first extra R reminds us to specifically ask about Relationships as well as for facts and figures.

∎ What is the coachee feeling?

∎ What is the emotional reality?

∎ Who else is involved and how are they feeling?

There is a real danger that managers will be tempted to skip the emotional realities involved!

The other R we add is for Resources, by which we mean what are the strengths and resources that will help the coachee to move forward. When have they been successful in addressing similar issues, for example? What are the resources and competences that will help them resolve the issue? You cannot focus simply on what the coachee cannot do!

Managers are often tempted to skip over the coachee's goal, and go directly to reality questions. Typically managers are very good at asking analytical questions concerning reality, but are not so good at asking about the emotional and psychological realities. As for options, the trap here is for the manager to give *their* options and opinions rather than ask the coachee for theirs. Many people also forget to ask about will and commitment, assuming that it will just somehow happen! It is important to ask specific questions about the degree of will and commitment and to get specific actions and dates and to follow up on these.

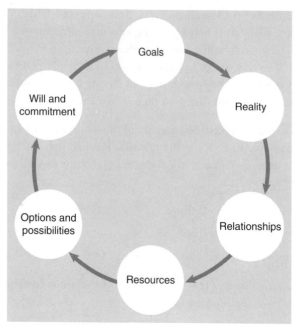

FIGURE 15.2 GRRROW model

OSKAR Model

The second model we find particularly useful is the OSKAR model developed by Solution Focus experts Mark McKergow and Paul Z. Jackson. This model incorporates solution-focused ideas on coaching, that is, the model focuses on looking for solutions rather than focusing on problems. It stands for:

Outcome — what does the coachee want and what would that be like?

Scaling — where are they now and what's got them there?

Know-how — what's working already?

Affirm and action — appreciating what's working, and defining what the incremental 'next steps' might be?

Review — noticing what's better and how did they make that happen?

- **Outcome** – the coach starts off by finding out the coachee's desired outcome. This is possibly an even better question than simply asking for goals. Many of us don't have a specific idea of what our goals are in a particular situation, but being asked about the outcome forces us to reflect on what we would like to achieve. This in itself would be a good coaching session even if we didn't get any further. The coachee would then have a much clearer idea of what they wanted.

- **Scaling** – this means finding out where the person is in relation to the desired outcome on a scale of 1 to 10. So, for example, if my outcome is to have a better relationship with my boss then the question would be, *'Where on a scale of 1 to 10, with 10 being high and 1 low, would you say your relationship is right now?'* If the coachee answered that it is a 3 out of 10, for example, the next question would be, *'Where on the scale would you like it to be?'* To which the answer might be a 5. From this you

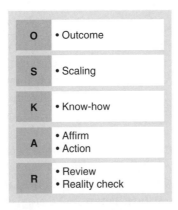

O	• Outcome
S	• Scaling
K	• Know-how
A	• Affirm • Action
R	• Review • Reality check

FIGURE 15.3 OSKAR model

Source: adapted from Jackson, P. Z. and McKergow, M., *The Solutions Focus: Making coaching and change simple* (Nicholas Brealey International, 2012)

would be able to ask what would a 5 look like or feel like? You could then ask specific questions about what your boss would be doing, or what you would be doing in a 5 out of 10 relationship. This forces you to imagine positive specific actions that you and your boss would be taking in this improved relationship. It also has the advantage of making you realise that you are not just a passive victim, but have an active role in this situation. It is not just about what your boss could be doing differently but also about what you could do differently. Once you are able to imagine what your boss could be doing differently, this allows you to ask your boss for specific behaviours that he or she can then respond to.

Know-how – this is about finding out what the coachee's strengths are. What resources do they have? When have they overcome a similar type of issue? Too often people see themselves as passive victims with no resources, but in fact it is very likely that they have strengths and resources that could be brought to bear on their current issue. Again the coach will help the coachee to focus on their resources and energy rather than their weaknesses.

Affirm and action – this is a two-step process. First, the coach will give a positive affirmation to the coachee. This is based on ideas around positive psychology that we discussed in Chapter 14. The coach will reflect back something positive that the coachee is already doing in the situation. This is important because it builds self-belief and confidence, but also, and importantly, it gives energy. It might be something like, '*I like the way you stood up for yourself in that difficult situation. It showed real strength and resilience.*' It's not easy for most managers to give positive affirmations but we feel that it is critically important to both notice people's positive behaviours and strengths, and above all to share them with the coachee.

The second step of the process for affirm and action is to ask the coachee in some detail about what specific actions they will now take to address the issue – the more specific the better. Don't allow generalisations; make sure you get very specific actions with time frames. If the coachee says, '*I'll talk to my manager*', that's not good enough. Ask them not only where and when, but more importantly *what* exactly they will say, and *how* they will say it. Get them to say it out loud to you so that you get a sense of how it might come across.

Again you might meet with some resistance here, but if you don't press for specifics then you are not helping the coachee to really think the issue through. As a matter of principle it is better to get the coachee to take a series of small steps rather than going for ambitious targets which they are unlikely to achieve. For example if you were coaching someone who does no physical activity you might want to hear them say they will start by taking a 15-minute walk every day rather than them tell you they will go from nothing to running five miles a day within a week.

Review – this can be done in two separate stages. First of all during the coaching session when you can look back and summarise what has been said, and then agree on specific actions and time frames. It is the time to ensure that you are both in agreement with what has been said and agree a time to meet up and review the actions. The second step in the review meeting is after the coachee has had a chance to implement their agreed actions. This is where you compare what the coachee said they would do, with what they actually did – and what happened as a result. This may lead to more coaching or a tweak in agreed actions plus any other follow-up plans. Think of it as a sort of reality check – what did they actually do and do they need to come back to Outcome and reconsider what they want to achieve and what is actually possible.

One of these five models can provide a useful starting point for any manager or leader in the early days of taking on a coaching role. However, we have found that as you become more experienced and confident as a coach you will find it more useful to develop your own approach.

Creating your own approach

The latest thinking on coaching is to move away from different competing theories and schools of coaching and back to the heart of coaching. According to research by our colleague Dr Erik de Haan, the essence of coaching is the quality of the relationship and using key skills such as effective questions, active listening, empathy and positive and constructive challenge all of which we have written about in the earlier chapters.

All these models and structures we share are extremely useful, but ultimately as a coach you have to have a process for coaching that works for you and be flexible enough to move and respond to the needs of the coachee and the situation. Remember that when you create your own coaching process, there are a number of basic requirements that will have to happen in most, if not all, coaching scenarios.

These are:

▌ **Issue Identification.** You need to find out what the issue and concerns of the coachee are. Here you will focus on being empathetic, listening carefully, including listening for emotions and allowing any emotions to be expressed. Be careful not to interrupt or try to give any advice here. Probe gently to make sure you are getting to the real issues.

▌ **Contract.** Here you need to know exactly what they are looking for. What do they want to get out of the session? How much time do we have? This is also the place to discuss confidentiality.

▌ **Goals.** This is a very important part of the process, and
one that in our experience is often overlooked. You cannot
really coach someone if they have not clarified their goals,
or what it is they are trying to achieve. We have observed
managers coaching others and asking good questions, but
what can the questions achieve if there is no clear goal?

So, be sure that the coachee identifies goals that are specific.
For instance if your coachee told you that their goal was
to be fitter, could you then go ahead and coach them? Well
you couldn't coach them effectively because when it came
to specific actions and follow up you would not be able to
refer back to any specific goals. So with our example we
would need to ask, *'What does fitter look like or feel like to
you?'* It is, however, quite difficult to achieve specific goals
immediately. Most of us don't go about with lots of specific
goals clearly etched in our minds. Although we do know
some managers who do! Most of us think in fairly vague terms
about what our goals around specific issues are. Coaching can
be extremely helpful here. So if you manage to help someone
clarify their goals and come up with some specifics we would
say that is already an effective coaching session.

▌ **Inquiry.** This is at the heart of the coaching process. You
need to help the coachee become more aware of their
issues, their reactions and other people's reactions to them.
What has happened? Who is involved? You need to ask
good probing open questions, be prepared to challenge the
coachee skilfully, and support where and when necessary.

This is also where you help the coachee to develop greater
understanding and awareness of their situation that is
critical to the success of the session. A trap managers often
fall into here is that they ask questions in order to better
understand the situation themselves so that they can give
the answer. Let us repeat here that the point of coaching
someone is not to ask questions so that you understand the
situation better; the point is for you to help the coachee

understand the situation better so that they have increased awareness and that they come up with their own answers.

▌ **Awareness of reality.** Since in coaching we are generally trying not to give advice and solutions to the coachee, we need to be able to sharpen the coachee's focus and stimulate their responsibility so that they have a better chance of coming up with their own solutions. Good, open questions can help do this, as can effectively challenging the coachee. This is a creative process where if the coachee reflects deeply on their issue they can start to generate ideas and possibilities. This creative part is critical and must come before the coachee can actually generate alternatives.

▌ **Development of options and alternatives.** This is where you ask the coachee what the options and possibilities are. But let's be clear, you don't give advice or suggestions here. A problem we often encounter is that when the coach asks the coachee what their options are, they respond that they don't know and might even ask you for advice here. Many managers can't resist stepping in and giving advice, but we would ask you to resist the temptation and not step in with any advice before you have elicited a reasonable number of options from the coachee. What is a reasonable number? The point is to get the coachee thinking for themselves so it depends on the context, but we could reasonably ask a coachee to come up with three or four options before we might think of offering any other possibilities. A good question to ask here is, '*What else could you do?*' Then remain silent to allow the coachee to reflect on the question. Then ask them once again, '*What else?*' followed by another '*What else?*' This forces the coachee to come up with more options than they could possibly do on their own.

▌ **Implication of these options.** During this stage you help the coachee think through the implications of their options. You can ask questions like, '*What would he say?*', '*How would she react?*'

▮ **Choice of option or options.** Ask the coachee to choose an action or course of actions. Don't let the coachee be vague and say something like, *'I'll talk to my boss'.* Ask them when they will talk to their boss, what exactly will they say and how will they say it!

▮ **Specific actions agreed.** At this stage you need to ask the coachee to commit to a specific action or course of actions. This means that you will ask them not only what they will do, but when they will do it and also how they will do it. The action has to be specific and measurable otherwise you will not be able to follow up effectively when you review the actions.

▮ **Follow up and review.** Having agreed a time and a place to do the follow-up you will then ask what the coachee has done, how they have done it and how successful it was. You will want to ask them what they will keep doing and if there is anything they want to modify. The process here is similar to what we have described above in the Evaluation step in the other models we have described.

We believe these ten points cover the main elements of a good-quality coaching session. Developing your own approach, model and process based on these will contribute to your professionalism and confidence as a coach. It will also enable you to give your full attention to the coachee as using your own coaching model is more likely to come naturally.

Tips for success

▮ Developing your own structure and process for coaching is by far the best approach.

▮ Use the models discussed in this chapter to help you develop and hone your own natural approach.

Coaching tools 16

As coaches ourselves, and in our role as management trainers, we run sessions to help leaders and managers develop their coaching skills. In both roles we use many different coaching tools and exercises to help these individuals reach effective outcomes. These tools will be useful for any coach to use appropriately as part of their coaching session with their coachee. In this chapter we offer you a selection of tools that you will find useful to draw upon when working with your coachee. The selection we offer are those we find most useful when working with our own coaching clients; however, this is not an exhaustive list. Rather it gives you a flavour of the sort of self-reflective exercises you can suggest to people as part of the coaching session.

These tools can be used for a variety of purposes:

▌ To help people reflect about an aspect of their coaching issue

▌ To offer a structure to the thinking process

▌ To give people reflective exercises between sessions

▌ To encourage people to think differently

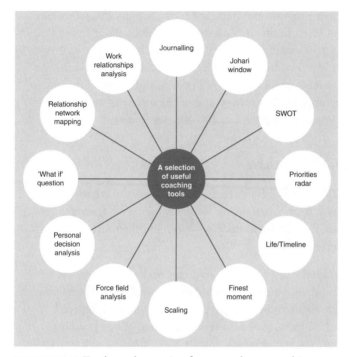

FIGURE 16.1 Tools and exercise for use when coaching

When using any exercise or reflective tool you must ensure it is appropriate for the actual situation and that the coachee is happy to use it, fully understands what they have to do, and how you will use it as part of their coaching experience.

In the remainder of this chapter we will examine each of the tools and give a brief description of how you could use it.

Coaching journal or diary

We always encourage our coachees to use a notebook during the coaching sessions. This notebook (or in the digital world an iPad or similar) will prove useful for your coachee to make general notes, but more importantly to keep a record of their progress and to record ideas, actions and reflections. In addition to this it is used to make notes about any of the reflective exercises that you encourage them to do. It also provides a reference point for future coaching sessions. The coaching journal should be a private and personal document used only by the coachee and not shared with anyone (unless of course the coachee chooses to do so).

Johari Window

Joseph Luft and Harry Ingham developed the Johari Window to help them when giving feedback to others. The model is a useful tool to help people understand themselves and how others see them.

The **open** window relates to things both you and others know about yourself. The **hidden** area relates to things you know about yourself, but you do not share with others. The **blind** area is about those things that others perceive about you, but of which you are unaware. The **unknown**

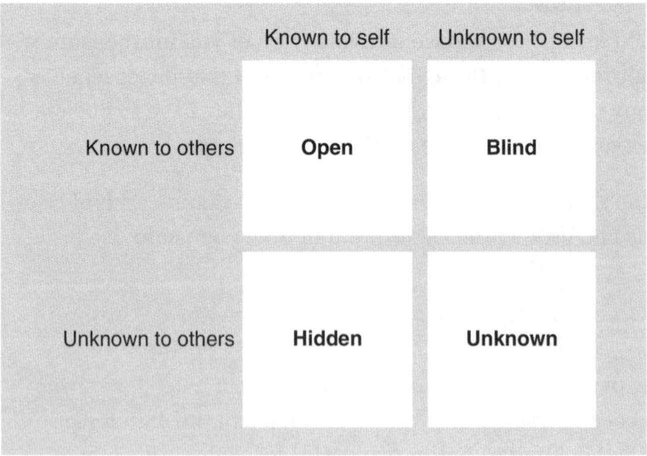

	Known to self	Unknown to self
Known to others	**Open**	**Blind**
Unknown to others	**Hidden**	**Unknown**

FIGURE 16.2 Basic Johari Window

relates to things in your unconscious which neither you nor others are aware of.

The idea of the Johari Window is that as a coach you can use it to help explore relational issues with your coachee. You can work together to review how large each of these panes is in relation to different people. Our colleagues Dr Erik de Haan and Yvonne Burger have adapted the Johari Window for use in coaching.

This can help you as a coach to be aware of what is being told to you openly by the coachee – this is the open space. What the coachee is not telling you is the hidden space. As a coach you will need to observe and pick up any cues and clues that are suggesting to you that your coachee is not revealing everything. If you believe this is the case you would then probe and explore with the coachee. In the blind spot the coachee is unaware, for instance, of the impact of their behaviour, of their feelings or emotions, or even

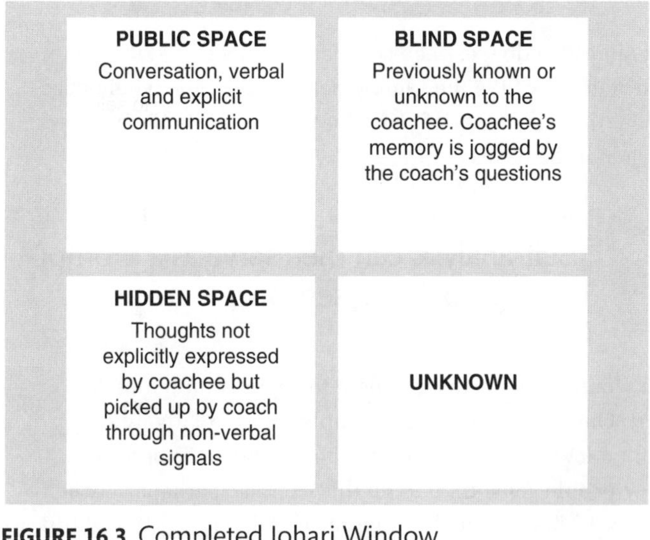

PUBLIC SPACE	**BLIND SPACE**
Conversation, verbal and explicit communication	Previously known or unknown to the coachee. Coachee's memory is jogged by the coach's questions
HIDDEN SPACE Thoughts not explicitly expressed by coachee but picked up by coach through non-verbal signals	**UNKNOWN**

FIGURE 16.3 Completed Johari Window

Source: Adapted from de Haan, E. and Burger, Y., *Coaching with Colleagues: An action guide for one to one learning* (Palgrave Macmillan, 2013)

memories which can be brought to surface and thus into consciousness through the coaching process. Of course, you must always be aware that your coachee may be making a conscious choice not to share everything with you and this must be respected by you.

SWOT analysis

This is a simple reflective exercise to encourage people to think about their Strengths, Weaknesses, Opportunities and Threats. It is often used as an early exercise when people are considering promotions or looking for a new job, or going through some other personal or career change. SWOT analyses can help the coachee to raise their self-awareness in relation to their strengths and weaknesses, but more than that to encourage them to think about the opportunities and threats that may happen by making a change. The self-analysis can then serve as a prompt for the coaching session to encourage the coachee to examine their view of themselves and the issue they are exploring.

It is simple to do – ask the coachee to draw a 2 × 2 box in their notebook (like the sample below) using the whole page so that there is plenty of room for them to write their views in each of the boxes.

> Self-analysis can then serve as a prompt for the coaching session

You would then encourage them to begin completing the chart. Our experience is that people find it relatively easy to put a few things in each box, but usually it is best to allow people some time to do this exercise perhaps between sessions! This will enable a more considered and thoughtful

Strengths	Weaknesses
(Things I am good at)	(Things I am not good at)
Opportunities	Threats
(Possible positive changes that will affect me)	(Possible negative changes that will affect me adversely)

FIGURE 16.4 SWOT analysis

analysis and give you more to work on when you come to review it during the coaching session.

Life/role priorities radar

Again this is a simple exercise to encourage people to reflect about the balance in their life. You might use this when someone is feeling overwhelmed, talking to you about a disparity in their life—work balance or in the balance of time they are spending on certain aspects of their job. The idea is to encourage your coachee to think about their life or their role holistically.

> Encourage your coachee to think about their life or their role holistically

There are three steps: first, thinking about what is going on for them at the moment; second, thinking about their ideal position; and third, thinking about the changes they may have to make to move towards their ideal position.

Ask them to draw a circle into their notebooks and to split this circle into segments annotating these segments with the main aspects of their life or current role. The example below uses typical life elements you may wish to consider, but you could use role specific elements, for instance client management, administration, team meetings, travel for business, etc. – whatever makes up the key elements of their role.

The challenge is to assess how much time or the level of satisfaction you feel about each of these elements. Using a scale of 0 to 10 (where the centre is 0 and the outer rim of the circle is 10) rate each segment marking it with a cross within the circle and then joining the marks to create a radar diagram of your current situation. Using a different-coloured

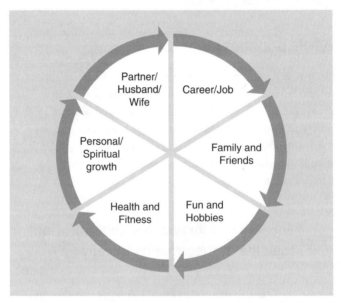

FIGURE 16.5 Life/role priorities

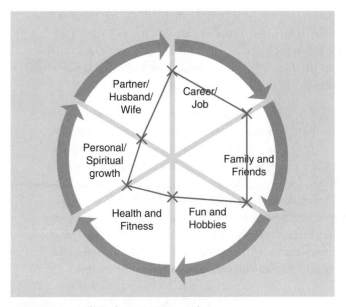

FIGURE 16.6 Life/role priorities radar

pen you can then do the same again, asking yourself what your ideal allocation of time or level of satisfaction would be. Once the coachee has done this you then have the preparation done for a discussion about what and how they would like to change to create better balance. See above for a sample of a completed life/role priorities radar.

Life- or timeline

This self-analysis exercise is used to help coachee's reflect about their life so far. This exercise is a useful way of encouraging someone to reflect about their whole life, or his or her time in an organisation or job role – depending upon the purpose of the exercise. It enables people to tell the story of the highs and lows using a single path. It can help your coachee to recognise achievements, challenges, to understand how experiences can be linked, to explore their responses to certain situations that will enable them to learn and move forward. Timelines are particularly useful when a person is feeling stuck in a rut or becoming despondent about their job or life in general, or in turbulent times when change is causing lots of uncertainty for individuals.

Again you need a notebook and/or a large sheet of paper. Stage one in creating your life- or timeline is to reflect about your life or time in the organisation or role and identify the highs and lows. In the coaching notebook make a list of the major events that have happened in your life or time in the organisation or role. Be sure to list those events that you consider to be both positive and negative. Now order these chronologically and annotate them with a '+' for the positives and a '−' for the negatives. After this reflective preparatory stage you can then create your timeline.

The timeline provides you with a pictorial view that can be more useful than a simple list as it can prompt people to see patterns or omissions. It also gives you the basis for analysis

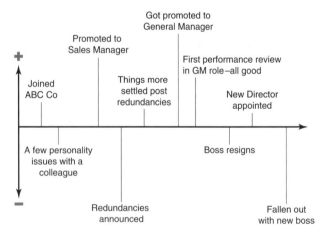

Timeline with ABC company

FIGURE 16.7 Timeline analysis

and discussion to review together and to identify what the coachee learned from each event and how they dealt with both the positive and negative events that might help them with the current issue. As a coach you can use this to explore several areas and ask many different questions, for instance:

▌ Can you talk me through your timeline explaining the major ups and downs?

▌ Can you identify any additional events that you may have omitted?

▌ Are your major events mainly issue or relationship driven?

▌ What did you feel at the time (for each event)?

▌ What patterns are becoming obvious?

Finest moment

This is an exercise we frequently use on leadership development programmes. Its purpose is to get people to think about a moment in their life when they have been proud of something they have achieved. It is a useful exercise to do with someone who is losing their confidence, demonstrating feelings of low self-esteem, demotivation or low morale. It can help them to focus on more positive times, re-energise the discussion and to draw lessons from the experience or event that can be applied to the current situation or topic under discussion.

Ask the coachee to think of a time when they have achieved something they are proud of or that stands out in their mind. Get them to describe in detail what the situation involved. Explore their motivation behind the achievement, get them to describe what was involved in detail including an exploration of their feelings during the event and finally get them to think about the lessons they can draw from this experience that could be applied today and in the future.

Scaling

This approach is written about more fully in Chapter 14 as part of the section on solution-focused coaching. The idea of scaling is that you encourage coachees to think about their issue and rate themselves on a scale of 1 to 10 with one being low and 10 being high.

So, for instance, let's say you are coaching someone who is having a problem with a colleague. You can use this technique to begin a conversation about improvement. Ask the coachee to rate their current relationship. They may say a 3 out of 10, so then ask them why they say this. Once you have discussed this you might then ask them where they would like the relationship to be – they may say a 7. Jumping from a 3 to a 7 can be a tall order so then you can ask them to think about how they might move incrementally from 3 to 5 on their journey towards 7. Encourage the coachee to identify specific actions they will take to improve the relationship. One of the major benefits of scaling is that it enables the coachee to see a path towards improvement by making small changes that will contribute towards the goal.

Force field analysis

This is a useful visual technique to help an individual to think through decisions in times of change. It encourages you to think first about the pros and cons of the decision, and then to help you analyse and communicate your rationale for your decision. Social psychologist Kurt Lewin first used this approach in the 1940s.

Let's imagine you are helping your coachee to decide about taking on a project overseas. The first stage is to be clear about the objective and to write it down. Then note down all the forces going for the change and then all the forces going against the change. Once they have done this initial thinking, they then create the force field analysis by drawing a rectangle in the middle of the page, then list the forces going for the change on the left hand of the box using longer or shorter arrows to indicate the importance of the force. Then list the forces going against the change on the right, again using the length of the arrow as an indicator of the importance of the force. Figure 16.8 sets out an example of a force field analysis.

A force field analysis can be done interactively during the session or by the coachee alone – doing it together may be particularly appropriate if you are the coachee's boss or have some knowledge about the issue at hand. Take care not to lead them to your own decision, but rather prompt them with questions to encourage them to think about the various factors that will influence the change, don't simply offer your opinion.

Take care not to lead them to your own decision

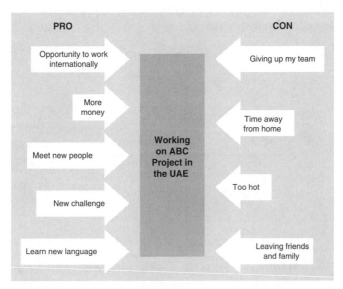

FIGURE 16.8 Force field analysis

Personal decision analysis

This is a simple yet effective tool for helping people to make decisions, especially in relation to two possible outcomes; for instance, if you are working with a coachee who is trying to decide whether or not to move from a branch office to head office as part of their career progression. Draw a 2 × 2 box on to a sheet of paper (or even on to a post-it note) and annotate the horizontal axis 'move' at the top and 'stay' at the bottom, and the vertical axis + on the left and − on the right. See the example in Figure 16.9.

Once you have drawn the framework then ask your coachee to complete the four quadrants with the positives and negatives relating to each option. You might ask them to think about the main benefits of moving and then list them in the top left quadrant with the disadvantages listed in the top right quadrant, and so on. This then gives a good start point for exploring the decision in more detail and can be extremely beneficial to help your coachee structure their thinking, to achieve clarity about the decision they have to make and to see their rationale.

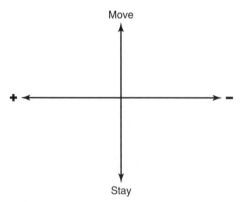

FIGURE 16.9 Personal decision analysis basic model

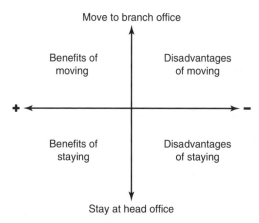

FIGURE 16.10 Personal decision analysis sample

'What if?' question

The 'what if?' question helps individuals to remove barriers to thinking and to encourage creative and positive thought. The idea is that if a coachee is struggling with an issue and can only see problems, a question that removes the problems and barriers from the discussion can help them to see other possibilities. Suggest to your coachee that you are going to try something different to get them unstuck and that this will require them to suspend judgement and do a bit of make believe. Then ask a 'what if?' question which would go something like this, '*What if the colleague you are having problems with today arrived at the office tomorrow and those problems had disappeared, what would that feel like? What would be different? What would the colleague be doing that would be more acceptable?*'

This is a similar technique to the miracle question we discussed in Chapter 14.

Some people find this technique difficult to get to grips with and you may need to help them further by prompting, for instance, '*Don't overthink this just give it a go. What would*

you like things to be like? Describe it?' Once the coachee
has spent some time describing their ideal to you, it will
of course be necessary to follow up with more questions to
determine what he or she can do to move towards this ideal.

Relationship network mapping

When coaching a colleague there will often be much
discussion about the people your coachee interacts with,
and helping them to deal with their challenge sometimes
involves relationship issues. We find creating and working
with a relationship network map to be very useful for both
the coach and coachee.

This technique involves using mind-mapping principles to
create an image of the people in your coachee's relationship
network. So it might look something like that set out in
Figure 16.11.

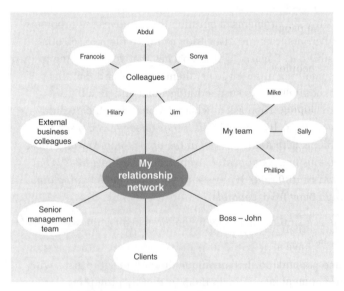

FIGURE 16.11 Relationship network map

Of course for most of us it would be rather more complex with many more named people, but this gives you an example of how your coachee might construct their own chart.

The relationship network map can be used for several different purposes during your coaching sessions, for example:

▮ To help you (the coach) understand the various business relationships your coachee is involved in.

▮ To help you to understand the position, impact and interrelationships between various people in the coachee's network when discussing different relationship issues.

You can also ask the coachee to annotate this map in all sorts of different ways as part of a relationship network analysis, for instance:

▮ Those people who are most important for your coachee's success in their role.

▮ Those people the coachee has a good-quality relationship with.

▮ The people the coachee finds challenging.

▮ The people the coachee feels would be worthwhile developing a better relationship with.

▮ The people you wish to prioritise if you are trying to influence them about something.

When we use this exercise with our coachees and with our programme participants the feedback we get is that it is a real eye opener in that many people had not previously thought their relationships to be as numerous or as complex. People have also told us that this process helps them to prioritise and structure their influencing and relationship development conversations so that they can be more productive.

Work relationship analysis

This analysis is a good way of helping your coachee to describe their work-based relationships, to explore the quality of each relationship based on 2 dimensions – work need and social need. For example, work need is where it is necessary for you to have an effective working relationship with an individual. Social need is where you choose to socialise with an individual. Looking at your relationships in this way can help your coachee to identify those relationships that work and those that require development.

It can also be used in conjunction with the relationship network map to assess each relationship.

So, first draw a 2 × 2 box on to a sheet of paper and annotate it as per the example in Figure 16.12.

The idea is to use the analysis to assess the quality of each work-based relationship or possibly one or two specific relationships that the coachee is having problems with.

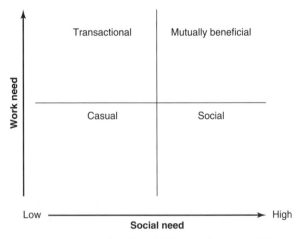

FIGURE 16.12 Work relationship analysis model

Each quadrant on the chart describes, in a general way, how the coachee might describe the relationship with a person:

▌ **Transactional** is a relationship where a person is important for the coachee's work but not particularly important as a social relationship. This may be a colleague who you know and is important to your effectiveness in the job but whom you choose not to socialise with.

▌ **Casual** are those relationships where there is little work need and you don't particularly have a social relationship with them either. These people are often on the fringes of your relationship network and may be more junior or provide an occasional service for you.

▌ **Social** relationships are with the people you enjoy being with. You like their company and may use them as a sounding board or devil's advocate when you want to share problems and challenges with someone. However, there is very little direct work need for the relationship.

▌ **Mutually beneficial** are those relationships where you have both a high work need and a high social need. These are people you like, trust and work well with.

> Use the analysis to assess the quality of each work-based relationship

Once you have positioned people on to the chart you can then use it as the basis for a discussion about why your coachee has positioned the relationship where he or she has, and what the implications of this are. Also, ask if there are any relationships that he or she would wish to move from one quadrant to another or to adapt in some way.

The aim is not to get all your relationships into the mutually beneficial quadrant (this would be unrealistic); rather it is to understand more about the quality of each relationship to help your coachee to develop effective action plans during coaching sessions.

Some of these tools relate and link to other processes and models in this book, while some have been developed and used by others and ourselves in our training and coaching practice, and some are well-publicised ideas for use in self-development.

The vital issue in using any tool during a coaching session is to be sure it is appropriate for the person being coached and the topic under discussion.

Tips for success

▌ Use appropriate tools, techniques and exercises to support your coaching discussions.

▌ Ensure your coachee fully understands the purpose of any tool used.

▌ Develop new tools and exercises that work for you and your coachees.

Part 4

Coaching scenarios

In this part we will look at a range of common coaching scenarios. In each instance we will offer ideas and suggestions about how you might approach each of the following scenarios.

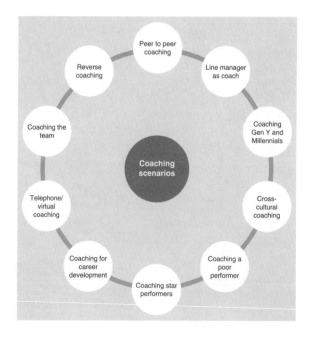

Coaching scenarios

Peer to peer coaching
Line manager as coach
Reverse coaching
Coaching Gen Y and Millennials
Coaching the team
Cross-cultural coaching
Telephone/virtual coaching
Coaching a poor performer
Coaching for career development
Coaching star performers

Peer to peer coaching

Peer to peer coaching (or co-coaching) is a process whereby two colleagues work together in a coaching partnership, both acting as coach and coachee. Peer to peer coaching is a great addition to anyone's professional and personal development. This technique is often used during management development programmes and, in our experience, participants always find it enjoyable and beneficial. The same, if not more, benefit can be gained from peer to peer coaching in the workplace. Once established it is an excellent process for continuous on the job development.

There are some major benefits to be gained from being involved in a peer to peer coaching relationship, these include:

▌ It enables you to be coached and to provide coaching to colleagues, who have similar experience to your own, know the organisation culture and some aspects of your situation.

▌ It provides you with a sounding board when you feel you need assistance with issues at work.

▌ It is extremely cost-effective as a development process as it only draws on the experience and skill of the two parties involved and is done in real time.

- It can contribute to developing a collaborative and facilitative organisational work culture.

- If adopted by senior managers and leaders, it may reduce the feelings of isolation that are frequently felt when promoted.

- It encourages executives to develop mutually trusting relationships where they are sharing experiences and knowledge.

- It helps you to develop your skill as a coach that can then be used in other coaching relationships.

- It enables you to work through real-life challenges and problems, and develop ideas with a trusted colleague.

- It models behaviour for other colleagues and your reports.

- It can be done face-to-face or virtually using one of the many conferencing technologies now available – skype, webex, etc.

> It enables you to work through real-life challenges and problems

Typically peer to peer coaching is done in one of two ways:

- One to one peer coaching
- Peer coaching groups

Both ways use coaching skills as described earlier in this book, however setting up and moving forward with these methods involve different processes.

One to one peer coaching

This is often a less formal approach to coaching and is certainly something individuals can do between themselves without organisational support. A process for establishing a one to one peer coaching relationship involves:

▌ Identifying a partner who you trust – this, of course, must be a mutual feeling between both parties. Talk to that person and explain why you think a peer coaching relationship with them would be beneficial. Apart from the fact that you believe you have a mutually trusting and open relationship with them, other possible reasons might be:

– they have similar challenges to your own

– you both have specialist business skills that you believe could prove to be mutually beneficial from a developmental perspective

– you have different experiences from one another and therefore you believe you could learn from each other

– you do the same job but in different regions, areas, countries, etc.

▌ Gaining their agreement to the relationship and discussing your ground rules and the process you wish to adopt. Possibilities concerning these rules and processes could include:

– it is essentially a helping and learning relationship rather than an advising one!

– it should be reflective and questioning, but not evaluative

– the need for confidentiality

– the need for a process – either on a need to meet basis, or what is more effective is to set a meeting at regular intervals and allocate enough time so that both parties can be coached during a session.

▌ Setting up the first meeting date and agreeing how long you will meet for and whether you will focus on one person or split the time between the two of you. You should also think about the venue, making sure it is appropriate and acceptable to both parties.

▍ Finishing the coaching session with a brief review of what worked, what didn't and what you will do differently for next time. Finally you should diarise your next meeting dates.

Peer coaching groups

This approach is where a small group of peers – usually up to five people works best – agree to work together on a regular basis to work through issues and co-coach one another in a peer to peer learning situation. Sometimes these groups are also called Action Learning Sets. Peer coaching groups are often adopted as part of the follow-up to a development event, or between a group of people who do a similar job but in different parts of the business. It is essential when establishing peer to peer coaching groups to contract and gain commitment within the group to agree:

▍ How you will work.

▍ The coaching approaches you will use – the approach generally used is to focus on one member at a time who will share their issue with the group and the role of the group is to use good coaching behaviour (as detailed in previous chapters) to help the group member work through their issue and leave the meeting with new ideas and an action plan.

▍ The timing of meetings – both frequency and length of each meeting.

▍ Any note-taking protocols.

▍ Confidentiality.

With peer coaching groups there are two common processes adopted:

▮ One process involves allocating an appropriate length of time – up to 1.5 hours – and focusing on one member during that time then rotating it round the group

▮ The other common process is where you allocate about 3 hours and each member takes their turn with the time allocated evenly between members.

Both processes work well and much will depend upon the preference of the members.

Peer to peer coaching provides everyone involved with a major opportunity to expand their skills, learn together and develop solutions to real-life problems.

Tips for success

▮ Peer to peer coaching helps to build your skill.

▮ Model coaching behaviour in your organisation by taking part in peer to peer coaching.

▮ When working one to one, do it with someone you trust and respect. Remember, this is a developmental relationship requiring openness.

▮ When working in peer coaching groups be sure you are all committed to the agreed process.

The line manager as a coach

Being a line manager who adopts a coaching style as part of their day-to-day managerial practice is probably one of the most common scenarios you will face. In order to be successful as a 'line manager as coach' you must create the environment, demonstrate the skills, build relationships with your people and develop a reputation as someone who is genuinely interested in other people. People will make their decision on whether or not they want to be coached by you based on your behaviour and how you relate to others in all your day-to-day dealings with them. This means that if you are truly committed to coaching as part of your managerial philosophy you will need to genuinely demonstrate this behaviour all the time. Consistent behaviour is important.

As a line manager coaching one of your direct reports there are, of course, a number of challenges you will have to be aware of:

▌ As you are in a position of authority they may simply tell you what you think you want to hear; or worse, they may even tell lies.

▌ The conversation could simply be at a superficial level because they are afraid to tell the truth for fear of negative consequences – *'If they don't trust they won't tell.'*

▌ The importance of total confidentiality.

▌ Being non-judgemental, meaning that in a coaching scenario you may explore issues that affect a person's performance in their day-to-day role. It is important to be able to remain objective and to decouple what you hear during coaching from a performance review discussion.

Consistent behaviour is important

As a line manager, there will be two circumstances in which you typically coach people. First, when one of your reports initiates the discussion where, for example, they ask for help, or they are experiencing a problem with a colleague. This is the easier of the two circumstances as the coachee has shown a desire to be coached by you. The second circumstance is when you perceive an issue where you believe they need coaching. This is more challenging, as your first step will be to persuade the coachee that there is an issue on which they need coaching. Do not start by telling them they need coaching. Start by gently asking questions to establish their view of the situation. If you are lucky and they recognise that they have a problem, then you can suggest you work together in a coaching conversation. If they still don't accept that there is an issue then ask them a more specific and detailed question about the issue you perceive. If they still don't recognise the issue, then the time has come for direct feedback and informing them of the need for a coaching session.

Do not start by telling them they need coaching

Tips for success

▪ Listen first.

▪ Show you are interested.

▪ Don't interrupt.

▪ Don't judge.

▪ Avoid saying things like, '*If I were you . . .*', or '*Why don't you . . .?*'

▪ Be appreciative of efforts the coachee has already made.

▪ Ask open questions.

▪ Try and get a bit deeper so you understand more.

▪ Show empathy.

▪ Focus on understanding, probing questions and moving to specific actions.

▪ Make sure any goals are specific.

▪ Ask your coachee to summarise their next steps and their timeline.

▪ Agree when you will next meet.

Coaching Gen Y and Millennials

People want to work with you now rather than for you.
Those are tiny words but a big distinction. I think the
command and control model is probably over.

Sir David Bell, former Director of People at Pearson Publishing

Definition of Gen Y and Millennials

It is perhaps appropriate to start this chapter by attempting
a loose definition of some of the terms used when talking
about different generations. The term 'Baby Boomers' relates
to the generation born in the years following the Second
World War from 1945 to 1960. Generation X refers to the
generation born roughly between 1961 and 1981, and is
followed by Gen Y (often also known as Millennials as they
enter the workforce post-2000) who were born somewhere
between the 1980s to the mid-90s. It is estimated that Gen
Yers now account for half of the employees in the workplace.
The next generation after Gen Y is Generation Z born
from 1995 onwards. They will be the most technologically
savvy generation ever. As baby boomers ourselves, we can
remember a time without mobile phones, computers and
colour TVs. Younger people laugh at us when we tell them
that there used to be only two television channels in the UK
and that programmes finished with the National Anthem!

> Gen Yers now account for half of the
> employees in the workplace

What do Gen Y want?

Gen Y and Millennials want fulfilling work, flexibility,
the opportunity to make friends and to connect to a larger
purpose. They also want a good salary, expect to be
promoted, want work–life balance and to be coached and
mentored!

In a sense that should make it easier for current mangers
to coach Gen Y and Millennials, because they are open
to coaching and actually want to be coached. Research
undertaken by Ashridge Business School shows that
56 per cent of UK graduates want to be coached or mentored.

> 56 per cent of UK graduates want to be
> coached or mentored

Interestingly, the research showed that more women Gen
Yers wanted a coaching/mentoring relationship from their
managers (61 per cent) than men (48 per cent).

The authors of the research wonder if this reflects a
gender preference among women for a more collaborative
and cooperative form of work and more openness to the
emotional and self-awareness aspects of coaching. However,
the fact that they expect to be coached can also make it
difficult for current managers because either they do not
coach Gen Yers, or they think they are coaching them but in
fact are really only giving them advice.

Another key aspect from the research is that Gen Yers do not have a strong sense of loyalty towards organisations. Members of Gen Y tend to stay in a job for about two to three years; often the reason they leave is unmet expectations of their work. Perhaps a strong culture of listening, coaching and reverse coaching would help them to stay on longer?

How to Coach Gen Y

One very interesting fact to come from the Ashridge research into Gen Y in the United Kingdom, was that 75 per cent of managers think they are coaching Gen Yers, but the Gen Yers themselves think that only 26 per cent of their managers are actually coaching them! So there is a real discrepancy between what managers and Gen Yers think coaching actually is. Interestingly, the same gap was evident in the Middle East, India and Malaysia.

At the risk of repeating ourselves, coaching is more about listening and questioning than about giving advice. You may feel that giving Gen Yers the benefit of your hard-won experience is a positive thing, but if you do, be aware that you are not actually giving them the coaching/mentoring experience that they want. So Gen Yers don't really want to hear advice from you, but they do want feedback. They are open to feedback, but want to have it in shorter bursts and in a more straightforward way than you are perhaps used to giving.

Coaching Gen Yers will be more informal, more relational and more value-based than you may have experienced when coaching older generations. You might also expect them to want to give YOU some feedback and coaching **(we talk about the concept of reverse coaching in Chapter 26)**. We can learn a lot from the Gen Y perspective and it would be arrogant not to listen to them and accept that they could also reverse mentor and coach us.

We can learn a lot from the Gen Y perspective

Gen Yers do not necessarily feel that they are well managed. A third (32 per cent) feel the way they are managed is below or greatly below their expectations, so as managers we would be well advised to get closer to the graduates and better understand their expectations of us as managers and leaders. We have said that Gen Y graduates want to be valued and respected, but 29 per cent responded that they did not feel valued or respected. Again, by doing more coaching and mentoring with the Gen Y graduates, we can show them the respect that they need, and also find out more about their needs and potential. Worryingly, 20 per cent are unhappy with the extent that they can use their abilities and knowledge in their organisations.

Cross-cultural Gen Y

The research tends to show that these findings are not limited to UK graduates but transcend national boundaries. That is, Gen Yers have more in common with each other than with national stereotypes. Research undertaken by Ashridge in the GCC countries in the Middle East shows that Gen Yers there also want a coaching style of management rather than a command and control one. In France, a recent study by the bank BNP confirms that Generation Z (the next generation that you'll be coaching) also want a flatter hierarchy, a coaching style of management, flexibility, work–life balance and a sense of purpose and meaning (BNP Paribas 2015). Again, Ashridge's research shows that Middle Eastern, Indian and Malaysian Gen Yers also want a coaching/mentoring relationship rather than a directive style of management.

Gen Yers have more in common with each other than with national stereotypes

In summary, it is clear that Gen Yers (and Generation Z) want to be mentored and coached, and treated with respect. They want a very different style of management and leadership, one that echoes the words of Sir David Bell – they want to work *with* you, not *for* you.

Tips for success

▌ Be aware that Gen Y colleagues expect coaching as part of their development.

▌ Don't fall into the trap of giving advice prematurely.

▌ Gen Yers believe in equality so work with them; don't tell them what to do. They, more than many others, want to develop their own solutions and plans.

Cross-cultural coaching

20

oaching as an approach to managing and leading originated in Western cultures. However, with the increasing globalisation of organisations it is also being adopted by other cultures. As leaders and managers work in an international context, often away from their own country, they are finding that they must coach people from a wide variety of different nationalities and cultural backgrounds. We offer the following tips many of which are based on our own experience of multicultural coaching.

What you can do

▮ **Be curious.** Ask the right questions. Don't make assumptions about the other person's culture. Show that you are interested and ask about the culture and how they like to work. Above all, show respect for the culture in which you are operating.

> Don't make assumptions about the other person's culture

▮ **Think about expectations.** What are the cultural expectations of a leader? What are people's expectations of a coach? How formal or informal is the culture? If it is very formal then you might expect that a coaching style of leadership will be more difficult, at least initially. So if a coachee asks you for advice, for example, you might inform him or her that you are happy to give some advice but that you need to ask some questions first. That way you reassure the coachee that their expectations will be met, while also having the opportunity to encourage them to reflect about the situation by first asking some open questions. Over time the questions can go on a little longer, and gradually as you develop mutual trust, you may find that they accept your coaching style more readily. We have run coaching sessions for managers in countries where we have been told that using a coaching approach is difficult, but in our experience we have found that the approach was generally welcomed and felt to be useful. The key is to take a step-by-step approach and not try to impose a style that is unfamiliar.

- **Explain what you are doing.** We think that it is also important to explain the coaching process in a rational way, and not to just start coaching people without letting them know what that actually means, or explaining the purpose of coaching. You have to be clear that coaching is perhaps a different way of thinking and managing, but that it has a clear purpose in helping people's development. If possible, make links to the culture you are coaching in. In China, for example, Confucian culture might value the leader's wisdom, authority and advice. This might lead Chinese employees to expect to be told what to do and to defer to the leader's decision. But if you explain what you are doing by asking questions and reassuring people that you can and will give advice, but only if necessary, then that might help convince people about the benefits of a coaching approach.

- **Show humility.** It is sometimes the case that managers from one country can appear to make the assumption that their culture is somehow better or more advanced than the one in which they find themselves. It isn't, it's just different. Telling people how it's done better back home isn't helpful. Of course it may be difficult working in a different environment; some of the values and working practices may be frustrating, but showing empathy and patience will be noticed and appreciated. Focus on the quality of the relationship between yourself and your coachees, even if you do not understand everything that goes on or why.

▌**Recognise differences.** You probably won't know all the differences between your own culture and all other cultures, but there are frameworks you can use to help you identify possible differences. For example, Dutch researcher Geert Hofstede's research originally came up with four dimensions, to which he later added another two dimensions.

The original four dimensions are:

— Power distance

— Individualism versus collectivism

— Masculinity versus femininity

— Uncertainty avoidance

The two latest dimensions are:

— Long-term versus short-term orientation

— Indulgence versus restraint

Power distance is about inequality or the way power is perceived. High power distance means that the boss, for example, considers themselves different to workers. He or she has a higher status, more power and so the culture is more autocratic. Low power distance cultures have more equality, bosses don't see themselves as being different and they would have less formal power. In a high power distance culture people are unlikely to openly disagree with people higher up in the hierarchy. In a low power distance culture, however, it would be quite normal to challenge the boss. In one multinational company that we worked for, the European vice president in charge of an Asian country told us that one of the key challenges he faced was to get his subordinates to tell him the truth. His experience was that employees would never tell bosses the bad news. When asked how things were going he was always told, *'Things are fine'*, or *'No problem!'* The culture was such that it would have been impossible to give a local boss bad news, but the VP actually wanted and needed his people to tell him the bad news as well as the good news.

Individualism versus collectivism is about the degree of dependency on other people and how individuals are integrated into groups. Collectivist cultures have a high degree of dependency and integration, and individualistic cultures a low degree. In individualist cultures, ties between individuals are generally quite loose, whereas in collectivist cultures, people are integrated into strong cohesive 'in' groups. For example, the United States is considered an individualistic culture, while Arab and Eastern countries are generally collectivist. This can affect the way organisations work, with the focus being more on the individual contributor in the United States, and on the group or team in collectivist cultures. This might imply that as a coach you would have to take into account the power of the 'in' group that the coachee belongs to far more than in an individualistic culture.

Masculinity versus femininity is about gender roles within a culture. The masculine culture is about assertive values, whereas the feminine culture is about caring values. Are the values in the culture you are coaching more masculine or feminine? If they are masculine values then the coaching approach could be perceived as a weak approach, but might be more readily accepted in a feminine culture. Another aspect to look at is the way you might choose to coach others in each of these cultures. You might, for example, find it easier to get a response to a question about emotions in a feminine culture.

Uncertainty avoidance is about the degree to which a culture is at ease with ambiguity. A high uncertainty avoidance culture is one that doesn't tolerate ambiguity well, whereas a low uncertainty avoidance culture is one that accepts ambiguity more readily. This can be important for coaches to be aware of. It is likely that a coaching approach that is based more on asking questions than giving answers would be more difficult to implement in a high uncertainty avoidance culture.

Long-term orientation versus short-term orientation as its name suggests is about the time perspective that a culture has – do we look at the short-term and immediate results or take the long-term perspective? Long-term cultures focus on virtues such as saving, persistence and future rewards. Short-term cultures tend to focus on the past and the present and on virtues such as respect for tradition, and fulfilling social traditions. The implications for coaching someone from a long-term orientation country might be that the coachee could respond better to questions about the future. The danger might be that if you are from a short-term orientation country you might focus too much on short-term issues when coaching.

Indulgence versus restraint is about how a culture looks at things like happiness, leisure, the degree of control over your life, and freedom of expression. So called indulgent countries score high on happiness, having control over your own life, and freedom of expression. High restraint cultures play down the importance of control over your life and freedom of expression. Again, the implication might be that you cannot assume that coachees in a high restraint culture will speak freely to you about any issues they have with their managers or colleagues.

Clearly your ability to coach and lead others, and how you do that, will be affected in some part by the culture within which you are coaching and leading. This is especially important when you as a coach come from a culture that is very different to the person or persons you are coaching. To give an example – if you are from a low power distance culture then as a coach you might assume that a person who is lower down the hierarchy from you would be comfortable in your presence and be prepared to speak up openly about any issues facing them. But if they come from a high power distance country their approach would be likely to be ill at ease and very guarded about what they say.

We have seen this, for example, on relations between managers from France and Sweden. French managers working with Swedes have told us about their frustration at the way Swedish managers make decisions. In Sweden it is normal to take time over a decision, involve everyone, discuss and challenge the ideas before finally coming to a consensus. This clearly takes time, and is what frustrated the French managers. The Swedish managers, however, thought that their French counterparts were too autocratic, too hasty in decision-making and didn't take the time to involve and listen to others.

As a coach, you need to be aware enough to understand, and flexible enough to adapt to, your cultural environment. What is interesting is that our research into Gen Y attitudes show that Gen Yers have a different approach to a coaching style of leadership than their parents. Even in cultures where you might expect a coaching approach to leadership to be difficult, our research into Gen Y attitudes has found that younger generations are often more open to coaching.

> You need to be aware enough to understand, and flexible enough to adapt to, your cultural environment

Another example is from India. Although India scores high on power distance, many of the country's best-run companies are using a coaching style of management. In a *Harvard Business Review* article entitled 'Leadership Lessons From India' (Cappelli et al. 2010) Indian leaders said that one of their key responsibilities is to be a guide, teacher or role model for employees. They spoke of a new approach, empowering employees by helping them find their own solutions.

Where is your country on Hofstede's dimensions?

It could be interesting if you are working cross-culturally to reflect on Hofstede's dimensions and see if there are any differences between your own culture and that of the coachee. You can read his books or consult his website at **www.hofstede.com**

For example, the following is a breakdown of the UK scores on each of these dimensions compared with other countries with significantly different scores (these are taken from Geert Hofstede's website).

Power distance

The UK scores 35 on power distance, making it a low-scoring country. Compare this with France, for example, which scores 68, making it fairly high on power distance and therefore a generally unequal society. Hierarchies are greater in France than in the UK and the approach in business is generally more formal in France than in the UK.

Individualism

The UK scores 89 on individualism, which makes it a highly individualistic culture. China and Japan, on the other hand, score 20 and 46 respectively. China is more collectivist than Japan, but Japan still scores much lower on individualism than the UK.

Masculinity

The UK scores 66 on masculinity, which is high and makes it a success-oriented and somewhat driven culture. To compare, let's look at Sweden which scores 5 on masculinity, which makes it a culture where feminine values (in general), such as caring for others and quality of life, are important.

Uncertainty avoidance

The UK scores 35 which is low and so makes the UK generally quite tolerant of ambiguity. To compare, let's look at Germany which scores high on 65, making it less tolerant to ambiguity than the UK.

Long-term orientation

The UK scores 51 which is an intermediate score. To compare, Japan scores 88, making it a country which has a long-term outlook.

Indulgence

The UK scores 69, which is high and makes the UK a culture which is oriented towards gratification and enjoyment.

Japan, however, has a score of 42, which makes it a culture where restraint is valued.

Remember that when coaching people from different cultures you may have to flex and adapt your style to suit your coachee.

Tips for success

▌ Ask questions and show curiosity.

▌ Be respectful of different cultures. Your way may not be their way.

▌ Be prepared to spend some time discussing and agreeing the benefits of coaching and the processes you will adopt.

▌ Flexing your style is vital when working in different cultural settings.

Coaching a poor performer

Managing and coaching a poor performer is challenging for any leader or coach, and is made even more difficult if the coachee is not aware that they are underperforming. There are some important elements to take account of when coaching someone who is not performing to their full capacity. In this short chapter we will highlight these and offer some ideas that will help you to deal with any coaching situation where underperformance is an issue.

Key considerations

When you are coaching someone for poor performance who is being termed a 'poor performer' it is worth considering the following questions:

- Is the underperformance a one off?
- Is the underperformance ongoing and part of a bigger issue?
- Is the coachee aware that there is an issue and actively seeking to sort things out?
- Is the coachee unaware?
- Is the issue ability, attitude or motivation?
- Are you the coachee's line manager?

these questions will tend to have an impact
ι approach the coaching session. On the one
e coaching someone whose performance has
ιed and he or she knows they have a problem,
ιιιυιι γ~~ be able to approach the issue openly and
encourage the individual to explain what's going wrong and
then work with them to improve matters. On the other hand,
if the individual is a habitual underperformer who appears
to be totally unaware that there is an issue you will have
a bigger challenge. Typically, in this situation you will be
a line manager who must first work with the individual to
help them to recognise and accept that a problem exists and
to identify what the problem is.

> Work with the individual to help them
> to recognise and accept that a problem
> exists

Guidelines for coaching poor performers

When coaching in this type of situation you will have to
draw on all your skills and capabilities as a coach. There are,
however, several specific guidelines that you should follow:

- **Plan your session carefully.** More than in any other
  coaching situation it is imperative to have a plan of
  action. Make sure you have thought through how you
  will start the conversation. Make notes about the specifics
  of the poor performance issue with examples, and the
  significance of these to the individual, the team and the
  business. Having all your facts to hand will make it easier
  to get to the point, stick to the point and help you plot a
  course to a positive outcome.

- **Make sure you have a private meeting space and
  sufficient time allocated.** Dealing with poor performance

requires your full attention, so ensuring you have a private space with no distractions is essential. There is always a possibility of the unexpected when talking about problem issues – you can never anticipate what is causing the poor performance so this sort of discussion can get quite emotional. Privacy and preparation will help you to deal with this.

▮ **Be specific about the behaviour you have noticed, the implications of that behaviour and give examples**. It is really important that you focus on behaviour the coachee can change and that you have actually experienced. So tell them what it is they have done and how this impacts on you and others. Don't discount by adding disclaimers, for instance, '*… and you are usually such a good member of the team'*. Be clear about what you want to say, say it and then give the coachee an opportunity to respond. So, for instance, let's say that you are dealing with someone who is in general a good performer but in the past few weeks you have noticed a change in their behaviour. You might say something like, '*Over the past few weeks I have noticed that your time keeping has become erratic and that some of the projects you are working on are getting behind. This causes me some concern as these projects are all important parts of a larger process and we need to complete them on time. Can we please talk about this and explore ways of remedying the situation?'* You have been clear about the issue and you have given the coachee an opportunity to give their perspective.

▮ **Don't make assumptions.** Poor performance can happen for many reasons – changes in attitude, lack of skill, something going on in the person's private life, etc. It is important that when coaching you give the coachee an opportunity to explain what's going on in their own words. You may be surprised and learn something about the coachee that you didn't expect. Remember, your role is to start with a positive assumption and work in an empathetic way to help the coachee improve their performance. Communicating this to the coachee early in the conversation can make things easier.

▌ **Adopt a businesslike and fair tone.** Think about how you manage the conversation. How you start things off will often contribute to the process of the discussion. So, keep your own emotions in check, don't make a big deal out of the issue, and be professional and businesslike.

▌ **Involve the coachee in finding a solution.** It is really important to involve the coachee in working the issue through and finding a solution. Once you have stated what the issue is you should quickly ask a question of the coachee and encourage them to share their views of the situation. Use the funnelling technique (see Chapter 6 on questioning) to ask an open-ended question, then follow it with a probe, then another, and another until you are satisfied that you have covered the issue in sufficient detail. The more the coachee is involved in developing ideas for improvement, the more committed they will be to the implementation plan.

▌ **Agree a course of action with goals, targets and review steps.** The main purpose of coaching a poor performer will be to reach an agreement together about an action plan for improvement. This should be stated very clearly together with plans for review and feedback along the way. At this stage it is worthwhile getting the coachee to summarise the action plan with detail about how they will implement the changes. It is also appropriate for you the coach to agree any resources or assistance for the coachee.

▌ **Be clear about the consequences of not changing.** It is only fair that you are clear about any consequences should the behaviour not change. These should be shared with the coachee.

▍ **Ask the coachee to summarise what they plan to do in writing and let you have a copy.** We find that asking our coachees to summarise in writing what we have agreed is good practice. First, it allows you to check that you both have a similar understanding of the situation; and second, once the coachees commit themselves in writing, it usually means they are more committed to the actions.

▍ Work in an empathetic way to help the coachee improve their performance

Coaching a poor performer is never easy but it can be incredibly rewarding to help someone to develop and improve their performance and to get back on track.

Tips for success

▍ Address the performance issue as quickly as possible before it becomes unmanageable.

▍ Start by inquiring openly about the situation rather than judging or blaming.

▍ Keep calm and businesslike and keep your emotions under control.

▍ Remember, it's the performance that's poor not the person.

Coaching star performers

22

Star performers and high achievers in general can be demanding of any coaching relationship. They are often people who have achieved significant success in their career or profession, whether that is in business, the arts or sports. Failure and mediocrity are not feelings they are used to, in fact really successful people often fear failure and find it difficult to deal with. This can make them tricky to deal with in a coaching relationship as they have high self-belief and high expectations. Any coach working with a star performer, no matter what the field is, will have to be credible and confident in their own right to build a meaningful, trusting and respectful relationship with their coachee.

> Really successful people often fear failure and find it difficult to deal with

In this chapter we will identify some of the reasons high achievers can be challenging to work with and will suggest ideas for building good-quality coaching relationships with typical star performers.

Behavioural traits

High achievers very often display some or all of the
following behavioural traits that can make them complicated
and challenging to work with. They are often:

- **Highly self-assured.** This is often displayed by their
  poise and composure in interpersonal situations. Their
  confidence in their own area of expertise is demonstrated
  by their knowledge, skill and capability in a wide range of
  different business settings.

- **Ambitious**. They have a strong desire for success and are
  usually highly motivated in whatever they take on, often
  to the extent of single-mindedness.

- **Competitive.** They can display a competitive spirit. Not
  necessarily with other people, but often competitive
  in that they want to beat the odds or improve on past
  performance. They may be keen to learn new skills and
  approaches to contribute towards even greater success.

- **Challenging**. They often think very quickly and adapt to
  new situations with ease and are driven to meet the high
  expectations they set themselves. They often approach
  their career and day-to-day work differently to their
  colleagues as they are always on the lookout for learning
  opportunities where they can improve themselves.

- **Goal driven.** They want to have stretching goals and
  targets so that they have the feeling of constant growth,
  development and achievement.

High achievers and star performers can also demonstrate
the darker side to their character in that if they overdo any
or some of the above characteristics they can appear to be
selfish, arrogant, confrontational, aggressive and possibly a
bit of a loner. Another danger that star performers can face
is the possibility of being derailed. Research shows that

there are several aspects of derailment that could apply specifically to star performers.

> Another danger that star performers can face is the possibility of being derailed

One is being *over* ambitious. Ambition itself is positive but there is a danger that some excellent performers set their sights too high. These are the performers who perform well but are not quite as good as they think they are! Other derailment factors are alienating people on the way up and thinking more about promotion than the job itself. There can be a tendency for star performers to think only of themselves and their personal goals and forget that they cannot make it alone. If they alienate colleagues on their way up, then there will be plenty of people to help them along when they are on their way down. Overreliance on one key strength, such as a natural talent, skill or pure energy, and in addition an overreliance on one particular sponsor or mentor, can derail a star performer. So when you are coaching a high achiever, it's worthwhile keeping derailment issues in mind so that you can be on the lookout for any potential derailers. Then help your coachee to recognise them as such and to work through ways of ensuring they don't fall into the derailment trap.

Thoughts to consider when coaching a star performer

Many of the skills, techniques and approaches already covered in this book will help you when coaching high achievers but the following ideas and tips may be appropriate to ensure a truly good-quality relationship. Star performers will expect their coach to be highly skilled and experienced and to work with them to further improve their performance.

This means that certain aspects of the coaching relationship will come into greater focus. These include:

▌ Relationship building and making a connection between the coach and coachee. The coachee will almost certainly expect the coach to demonstrate capability in the areas that they wish to focus on. So, for instance, if a coachee wishes to talk about how to handle fellow board members they would typically expect their coach to have had significant board-level experience themselves either as a coach for others or as a board member. There needs to be a good connection between the coach and the star performer at a personal level. Building trust and mutual respect will be paramount.

▌ Contracting to agree the focus and processes that you will adopt when working together. Features of a coaching discussion with a high achiever will be:

– Challening your coachee to continually explore, improve and develop. Focus on stretching them.

– Helping them to see the actual outcomes from the coaching sessions. Work with them to explore what has changed and improved and how they will continue to incorporate this into their day-to-day work.

– Being prepared to offer feedback, both positive and negative, about your perspective on how they are performing. Any negative feedback should always be accompanied by ideas to explore for improvement. Positive feedback should acknowledge their ability, skill and achievements.

– Being willing to follow their lead in terms of the agenda for any session. Have your antennae on high alert for cues and clues that indicate the coachee is ready to move on to something different. They tend to want a fast-moving discussion and may not feel the need to dwell on issues once they believe they have 'got it'.

— Being courageous. Some high achievers may have already achieved a lot, but they may not be quite as good as they think they are! In our conversations with top coaches from the world of sport we have learned that many successful performers have a somewhat inflated view of their capabilities. This also applies in the business world. Top performers often focus their efforts on very narrow criteria, for example they only focus on results and forget to take care of their relationships with their colleagues and support staff. This can result in them being regarded as somewhat aggressive and possibly regarded by some as a bully. This can mean that someone else may have to get involved to pick up the pieces. So, it is essential for any coach to be courageous and be ready and willing to challenge the coachee's opinion of themselves.

— Making your coaching session about the coachee's needs. They must feel that they are in control. Early on in the relationship you should explore what their dreams and ambitions are and how they believe a coaching relationship can help with this. The focus should be on the future.

— Not shying away from the difficult areas. It is important to help a high achiever identify any blind spots, overdone strengths or self-limiting beliefs – these are the areas that could trip them up at some point in the future. High achievers can and do plateau and some completely derail. Your job as a coach is to help the coachee avoid these possibilities.

> Be courageous and be ready and willing to challenge the coachee's opinion of themselves

Coaching a high achiever can be incredibly rewarding for the coach as it can test and stretch you as well as the coachee.

Tips for success

▌ Find out what the coachee's dreams and ambitions are.

▌ Ask them to talk about their strengths and then ask what the flipside of these strengths might be, and how these might come across to others.

▌ Be prepared to challenge your coachee and ask them if they could do even better.

▌ When questioning star performers, don't just ask about their own performance, ask about how it affects others.

Coaching for career development

Coaching people to help them develop their career is one of the most common reasons for a leader or manager to coach staff in their organisation. Helping a colleague to develop further and to fulfil their ambitions and aspirations is certainly one of the most rewarding aspects of any coaching relationship. Much of what we have covered in earlier chapters will be useful when coaching for career development; however, the following ideas will add value and help you to focus on career issues.

What is career coaching?

Your role will be to help and support your coachee to think about their career so far, and to assist them with the planning process for their future career development. As with any coaching relationship, career development coaching involves commitment on both sides. It is also worthwhile recognising that coaching for career development does not always mean promotion, but can mean increasing breadth and depth of your coachee's skills and capabilities so that they are better prepared for any possible career opportunities when they present themselves.

> Your role will be to help and support
> your coachee to think about their
> career so far

Making career decisions are among some of the most important decisions an individual will ever have to make, so your role as a coach in this context will be to help people to:

- Continue to be challenged, motivated and growing in their career.
- Reflect about what they have achieved so far.
- Understand how they have reached their current career stage.
- Explore possible career futures, dreams, ambitions and aspirations.
- Provide assistance by introducing them to the various tools and techniques that can help them to achieve their goals.
- Develop an actionable career plan with clear goals and stages.
- Keep on track with their goals by challenging, supporting and reviewing on a regular basis.

Areas to cover during a career development coaching relationship

A career development coaching relationship will probably involve you in a longer-term process than some of the other scenarios we have discussed. Of course this is up to the people involved, but we believe that in order to get the best out of this type of relationship be prepared for a relationship that might last for several months, even years.

> Be prepared for a relationship that
> might last for several months, even
> years

During your sessions you should cover some or all of the following:

▌ Review their career so far to help them identify what they have achieved, how they have achieved it and why they made the career decisions they made. Help them understand their strengths, development needs, motivators, blind spots and any patterns that can be identified that have helped in their progress or that have hindered it. Some of the exercises in the chapter on coaching tools may be useful here, for instance Johari Window, SWOT Analysis, Time- or Lifeline (see Chapter 16). During this phase you may also like to use a psychometric tool to help your coachee explore their strengths, weaknesses, development needs and preferences. There are many tools on the market, some of which are easily accessible using the internet – however, many require specialist training to administer and debrief, so you may require assistance here, possibly from your HR department. Psychometrics that often prove useful in this context are:

– Myers Briggs type indicator

– Strength deployment inventory

– Belbin team type questionnaire

– Career anchors

– Profiler or another generic 360° competence questionnaire

– OPQ – Occupational Personality Questionnaire

– Talent Q dimensions questionnaires

– Team management systems

– Hogan personality inventory

These questionnaires can provide you with a wealth of information and will add to the quality of any career development discussion. They can help a person to raise their self-awareness and to explore aspects of their career and skills in more depth.

▌ Spend time helping your coachee to think about the parts of their job that energise them and provide them with the most satisfaction. Using the 'finest moment' exercise can be useful here. It can also be beneficial to think about those things that the coachee dislikes about their current job. Understanding what currently engages and disengages your coachee can be a useful exercise in that it will help the coachee when making decisions about future roles or career paths.

▌ Explore with them their career aspirations. What do they hope to achieve in their career? Sometimes it is a good idea to work with timescales when discussing this; for instance, 'What are your aspirations for the next year, or five years?' Or, whatever seems appropriate for the coachee's current situation. During this exploration, no judgements should be made – allow the coachee to share their dreams and ideal career ambitions with you.

▌ Help your coachee to set career goals. The aim here is to make sure these are realistic and achievable. Once they have established their goals and a timeline for them, get them to think about how they will achieve them. What development will be necessary? What opportunities are available for improving, expanding and growing the skills and capabilities necessary to achieve their goals?

▌ Work with your coachee to regularly review any progress made against their goals. During this phase it is important to recognise that plans and goals change so you should also be prepared to help your coachee adapt and flex their plan to suit their circumstances.

Some useful career coaching questions

▌ What are your career goals and aspirations?

▌ Where do you see yourself in a year? Five years? Ten years?

▌ What energises and motivates you at work?

▌ What would you say you are passionate about?

▌ What achievements are you most proud of so far?

▌ Looking ahead, what would make this year a success for you?

▌ What do you see as your key strengths? Weaknesses? Development areas?

▌ What hurdles do you think you will have to cross to achieve your dreams?

▌ What have you learned in the past year that will contribute to your career success?

▌ How will you know when you have been successful?

▌ If money was not an issue for you, what would you do with your life? What does this tell you about yourself and your career?

▌ What do you like about your current job? What do you dislike about your current job?

▌ What would knock you off track?

Tips for success

▍ Actually make time to have these conversations – as they are not problem-based they often get forgotten. Development is the essence of coaching and helping others to grow is a coach's main role.

▍ Adapt the suggested questions to suit your coachee's situation.

▍ Recognise and appreciate their success and good work so far and be prepared to probe and challenge what else they could do.

Telephone and virtual coaching

I n our increasingly global world many people work in international contexts. This can provide an additional challenge for any coach. However, this also provides a great opportunity for the coach to develop their skills in a new area, that of coaching by telephone, teleconference or videoconference. Many of the skills used during face-to-face coaching are applicable when using telephone or virtual coaching; however, some skills will require greater focus and competence.

Pros and cons of telephone and virtual coaching

There are certain advantages to be gained from telephone or virtual coaching, these include:

▌ There is more opportunity to fit coaching around a person's work or travel schedule, which means that 'meetings' are often more focused, yet relaxed.

▌ There is more choice for both the coach and coachee as to where the coaching session will take place – often in the comfort of their own homes, which we find can add to the quality of the session.

▌ Shorter meetings are often a feature of telephone or virtual coaching as it can be difficult to concentrate effectively for very long periods when on the telephone. This can also mean that the coachee focuses more clearly on the issue and process, as there are fewer distractions.

▌ As listening skills are key to a coach's success when telephone or virtual coaching, it may be the case that with increased acuity in this area the coach will tend to pick up more than they might when face-to-face. Of course, this also provides you with a great development opportunity to hone your listening skills. With practice you become more attuned to the variation and discrepancies in the coachee's tone of voice. When coaching face to face you often focus on the visual cues and not on the auditory ones.

> ▌ The coachee focuses more clearly on the issue and process, as there are fewer distractions

The main disadvantage for telephone and virtual coaching is the absence of visual cues for both the coach and coachee to pick up on. This means that the coach must rely largely on their listening and questioning skills to ensure they are capturing all the data and nuances of the communication. Some people may also find that telephone or virtual coaching is not for them, as they prefer the intimacy of face to face so be sure to check with your coachees that they are happy to go down this route.

Ideas to consider

As a leader or manager who is coaching via telephone or some other virtual method it is highly probable that you will have met the coachee previously. For most of you the person you are coaching may be a direct report or colleague who has moved to another office or who is working out of their base office on a regular basis. This is unlike many professional executive coaches who can find that their coaching assignments are increasingly using telephone or virtual methods and they do not have the benefit of a face-to-face meeting at all.

To ensure success the following tips are worthy of consideration:

▌ Structuring and agenda setting are extremely important when telephone or virtual coaching. The coach and coachee must agree the plan for the session/s. This is important so that both parties can focus on the session objective and move towards agreeing actions and outcomes.

▌ Briefly summarising the previous session can be useful to remind both coach and coachee what has been achieved so far.

▌ Planning for these sessions is vital – both by the coach and coachee. We find it is beneficial for the coach to contact the coachee a few days before the planned session to remind them of the timing and to ask them to think about what they would like to cover and to let you know prior to the session so that you can plan in advance.

▌ Once you know what the coachee wishes to focus on, you can begin to structure the session and plan your inquiry process.

▌ Make sure that you won't be interrupted – switch off your telephone and any other technology that may interrupt you. Some coaches we know, who coach from their home, even put a notice in their front window saying that they do not wish to be interrupted.

- Make sure your notebook is at hand and it is also a good idea to have a glass of water.

- During the coaching process you should ensure that you check regularly that the coachee is on track and also to test your understanding by paraphrasing what you think they are saying.

- Due to the absence of visual cues it is important that you not only test understanding for the rational factual data being conveyed, but also ask how your coachee is feeling about issues being discussed.

- At the end of the session it is more important than ever to ask the coachee to summarise what has been agreed and how they will put the ideas into practice.

- Agree the next meeting date.

- We also find that an immediate summary email to your coachee, with brief notes of what you covered, any actions you agreed and the date of the next meeting is useful.

> Ensure that you check regularly that the coachee is on track

Telephone and virtual coaching are becoming a much more common way of undertaking and maintaining coaching relationships, so many of you may find that this approach is one you actively find in your repertoire or even want to add to your skill base.

Tips for success

▮ Make sure you are in a quiet place with no possibility of interruption.

▮ Try to have a hands-free set up. This will make note taking easier.

▮ Invest in good-quality equipment if you are going to be doing a lot of this type of coaching.

▮ Do your preparation and planning. This will help you get started even if you deviate during the conversation.

Coaching the team

*If coaching individuals has its difficulties and
complexities, then these are multiplied when coaching
teams.*

Myles Downey (2003)

Teams carry out most of the work in organisations. We
are all members of several different teams at any one
time and this is a fluid situation with teams constantly
evolving. Teams have different dynamics to individuals
and so we must be able to coach the team as a whole entity,
without forgetting to address the needs of the individual
members of that team.

Coaching teams in sport and teams in organisations

The most common type of team performance may be
in sports where teams feature heavily, and even where
the sport is an individual one like tennis there is still a
team supporting the individual performer. Are there any
transferable principles from team performance in sport to
team performance in organisations? We believe so. Ashridge
has worked with many sports teams and coaches over the
years and we will share our thinking with you; we will also
share ideas from sports coaches, managers and specialists
with whom we have discussed these issues.

Team coaching

European, Commonwealth and World champion sprinter and hurdler Kriss Akabusi says that the difference between individual coaching and team coaching is that the team coach would do the same as the individual coach, but also needs to look at team strategy, processes, systems and tactics.

As there might be less time for personal coaching in the team it should be more about processes and less about individual feelings and emotions. There may be an assumption in the team that each individual in the team already has a personal coach. The team coach would be looking at the individual's role in the team's purpose, strategy and goals. So in the team you need to be on the same page and heading in the same direction.

As Kriss puts it: 'It's less about me and more about us.' For the England Rugby Football Union's (RFU) head of Elite Coach Development, Kevin Bowring, there has to be an alignment of goals and purpose if a team is to be successful.

> You need to be on the same page and heading in the same direction

Transferable learnings

The key question then is what are the transferable principles from team coaching in sport to team coaching in businesses and organisations? According to research by Dr Mark Lowther of Cardiff Metropolitan University's School of Sport, the three key transferable principles of team coaching are context, process and contact.

▎ **Context.** This is about the wider climate in which both the team and individuals operate. It is essential to create a culture and climate that encourages and supports the goals of the team. As England Rugby's Head Coach Stuart Lancaster says, 'Culture precedes performance.' If the culture is wrong then performance will suffer. This is the same in business as it is in sports organisations, so the leader as coach needs to create the appropriate cultural climate in order for the team to perform effectively.

One example of creating an appropriate culture for the team is given by the RFU's Kevin Bowring. Kevin told us how Stuart Lancaster created a wider climate of respect, appreciation and purpose by writing to the parents of all the players in the senior England squad and asking them what it meant to them – the parents – for their sons to be England players. He also then asked the parents to ask the son's first coach or sports teacher what it meant for them to see their protégés wearing the England jersey. He then had the quotes framed and put them in an envelope and gave them to the players.

He also connected players with their first rugby clubs by having them run out on to the pitch during international rugby games alongside the mascots who were wearing the colours of the player's first rugby club. So this involved not only the players themselves, but the parents, sports teachers and rugby clubs who were all involved in making the player an England international. You can imagine how they all felt to be recognised in this way. So this can equally be applied in organisational coaching where you can easily ask team members what it means for them to be part of this team.

▎ **Process.** This is about developing a cohesive team and the processes that can be used to do this. As Nigel Melville, CEO of US Rugby, says: 'The best results come from me following a process and the person being coached not being aware of the process.' There are three subcomponents of process: relays, relationships and shared purpose. They are issues that the team coach has to be aware of and has to bring to the surface as they are very often ignored.

— **Relays.** One of the processes is to be able to use senior members of the team to act as a relay. If the team is large then you cannot realistically know what's going on with every member of the team. But the team members themselves can and do. So if you are able to have a subgroup of senior team members who are onside with your vision and approach, then they can act as substitute team managers and coaches in the sense that they will remind team members of the team goals, values and ways of working and reinforce the key messages. This is common in highly effective teams in the world of sport. For example, the former Liverpool FC and Scotland footballer Graeme Souness agrees that the idea of having the senior members of a team act as a sort of relay is critical. Writing in the *Sunday Times* (18 January 2015) he said: 'When I was at Liverpool the coaches very rarely had to say anything because the senior players would set the standards for everyone else.' As a team coach you cannot do everything, and unless you have senior members of the team, who are respected, relaying your approach then it will be difficult to manage a team effectively.

— The New Zealand rugby team, the All Blacks, the most successful team on the planet with a win ratio of 85 per cent, also use this idea. They have a leadership group within the team, composed of the captain and senior players, who role model and embed the values on a day-to-day basis. The point is that the coach is not enough. So when you look at your team, who are the team members who are respected and who can relay your message? This is especially important when the team is dispersed geographically.

– **Relationships.** Another important aspect a team coach will look at is the relationships between team members. For example, what is the level of trust between team members? What are the differences between team members; for example, what differences are there in ways of working, ages and expectations? Kriss Akabusi thinks that trust is critical. So what is the level of trust between you and the team and between team members themselves? As Kriss says, why would you listen to someone you don't trust or respect? So you may like to ask your coachees how much they are trusted by the team and follow that up with an exploration of how trust can be further developed in the team.

– **Shared purpose.** 'Talent without unity of purpose is a hopelessly devalued currency', said Sir Alex Ferguson (*The Independent*, 30 April 2011). It is critical to have conversations with the team about the shared purpose. This is not something that can be assumed, so there needs to be absolute clarity around that shared purpose. What does the team want and how will it get there? As a team coach it is your job to initiate and facilitate these conversations. If you don't then you are likely to find that despite talented individuals the team is always going to be less than the sum of its parts. In fact you may find that the different individuals are working at cross purposes to each other and actually sabotaging what you are trying to achieve.

▌ **Contact.** This is about managing individual talent. Although we are talking about coaching teams, we can't lose sight of the fact that the team is composed of individuals, and so, paradoxically perhaps, we need to be able to address the individual needs, issues, preferences and talents in the team. It is important not to lose sight of the individual and their unique personality traits and personal circumstances. While traditionally the focus of coaching was always about the team, the reality and complexity of modern group settings and squads requires a leader to both skilfully coach the team and actively connect to the player. Dave Brailsford of British Cycling and Team Sky calls this a rider-centred approach.

> The three key transferable principles of team coaching are context, process and contact

At the same time we need to be aware of team goals and any potential clashes between individual goals and team goals. So you need to be flexible to individual needs within the team and adapt your style to the needs of the team members. There is a popular saying, 'There is no I in team', and this has been widely accepted. But writer and researcher Dr Mark de Rond from Judge Business School tells us in his latest book that this is totally wrong and that there is in fact an 'I' in team (De Rond 2012). You have to address the individual components of the team as well as the team itself, otherwise the team will not function effectively.

Team coaching – the five disciplines

Peter Hawkins of Henley Business School has developed a useful and practical model focusing on three aspects of team coaching and five disciplines of team coaching. At the heart of the model are three essential aspects of the team:

- Task – the purpose of the team.
- Process – how the team will achieve its purpose.
- Relationships – this is looked at from two perspectives: internal and external.

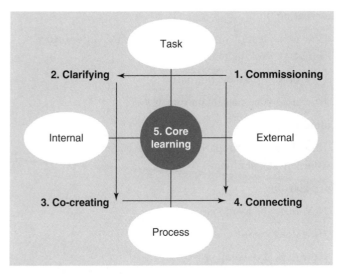

FIGURE 25.1 Team coaching – the five disciplines

Source: adapted from Hawkins, P., *Leadership Team Coaching in Practice* (Kogan Page, 2014)

Around these three aspects he has developed five key disciplines. For each of the five disciplines he suggests some useful questions you can ask when coaching a team.

▌ **Commissioning**

— Who does the team serve?

— What is its purpose?

— Why does it exist?

— How does this align with organisational objectives?

▌ **Clarifying**

— What is its collective task?

— What are the core objectives?

— Is the team clear about roles? Preferences?

— Is the team clear about working processes?

▌ Co-creating

- How is the team working together? How creative? How skilled at working together?

- How does it partner internally?

- How does it manage team dynamics?

▌ Connecting

- How does the team partner with the wider system and your key stakeholders?

▌ Core learning

- How does the team learn?

- How does it continue to learn?

- How does it develop as a team?

We suggest that you use these questions together with your own personalised questions to create better awareness of the essentials of team performance in the context in which you are operating.

Challenges of team coaching

The CEO of US Rugby, Nigel Melville, thinks that team coaching is more challenging as there are more parts and so many different personalities. Although he finds team coaching more challenging, he also finds it more rewarding than just coaching individuals. For him, the biggest challenge in the workplace is that it is often easier to tell someone what to do rather than encourage them to work it out for themselves. On the sports field, the players have to do it themselves, so just telling them is not enough – you can't do it for them!

Another challenge is actually finding time to coach the team. Nigel suggests that it is essential to make time to coach.

He recognises that this is difficult as there doesn't seem to be any time to practise (as you would do in sport), as in business, all the focus is on the next deadline, the next deal, or the next meeting. No doubt you have experienced the same issues as Nigel. So how then can you make sure that you do set aside time for coaching the team?

His suggestion is you need to either slow down the pace of the work, or develop a quicker coaching process that works for you. If not, you will not be an effective team coach, and your team's performance will suffer.

It is essential to make time to coach

Tips for success

▍ Remember, it's about getting the balance right between the team's needs and the individuals' needs.

▍ Remember the three key principles:

– Context – make sure the climate and culture around the team is right.

– Process – use trusted team colleagues as relays; ensure the relationships between you, the team and the team members' themselves are good; think about levels of trust.

– Contact – don't forget the individual.

▍ Successful team coaching builds trust, respect and helps develop peak performance.

Reverse coaching

This is a relatively new idea in the coaching world where a younger junior manager works with an older senior manager in a reverse coaching scenario. This innovative approach has tended to come about because of an organisation's clear commitment to coaching as part of their development philosophy. They have often received feedback from the younger managers that suggests that in the contemporary technologically driven world senior managers don't understand the younger generations, don't communicate with them and don't think like them. It was this sort of feedback from a staff survey undertaken in 2008 that encouraged Charlie Johnston, HR Director at Cisco UK, to design a reverse mentoring programme. Perhaps one of the biggest benefits of reverse coaching is the opportunity for learning to take place by both parties.

Benefits of reverse coaching

Organisations that have incorporated reverse coaching into their development strategy together with their senior managers and their more junior coaches have benefited enormously in a variety of ways. For the more senior managers these include:

▌ A chance to develop an awareness of 21st-century skills and the needs of their Gen Y and Millennial colleagues.

▌ An opportunity to gain an understanding of what motivates and demotivates the younger generation.

▌ A chance to learn new technological skills and their benefits; for example, using social networks, tweeting, blogging as part of their communication process.

▌ A way to show a genuine interest in listening to, involving and operating a top-down and bottom-up organisation.

▌ An opportunity to re-energise – it can be hugely motivational to work with someone who is at the beginning of their career and who can challenge senior managers' thinking and encourage them to look at the world through a new set of lenses.

> ## Gain an understanding of what motivates and demotivates the younger generation

For the younger managers the benefits include:

▌ An opportunity to have an official in-depth and open relationship with a senior manager who they would not normally have access to.

▌ A chance to develop their confidence and open their eyes to the challenges that come as you move up the managerial ladder to more senior-level appointments.

▌ An opportunity to provide opportunity for both knowledge and experience sharing.

▌ A way to gain a better perspective of the motivators and demotivators of the older generation.

For the organisation the benefits include:

▌ A chance to build greater loyalty and improve morale due to the feeling of being listened to and communicated with.

▌ An opportunity for cost-efficiency, as it is creating two-way learning channels encouraging managers who have different knowledge levels and experience to learn from each other.

▌ A way to contribute to talent management and succession planning processes.

▌ An opportunity to give the organisation an edge in that it will have employees that have a greater understanding of each other's needs, aspirations and motivations, thus making it a more enjoyable and effective place to work.

> ▌ A way to contribute to talent management and succession planning processes

It is also worth recognising that many young people are now successful and active in start-up businesses and some are already successful entrepreneurs. These people are very serious business people in their own right and have much to offer others in any coaching relationship.

As with any new idea there are, of course, limitations, challenges and hurdles to be aware of. However, if you involve open-minded people who are willing to work together in a committed and non-judgemental way, to challenge one another, to explore ideas and ways of working and to genuinely learn from each other, you will find that reverse coaching will be accepted more readily. Anyone taking part in a reverse coaching or mentoring relationship must go into it with an open mind. They must be willing to have some of their ideas criticised and challenged, and to explore new ideas and ways of doing things. One of the biggest hurdles can be that the more senior manager finds it difficult to have the less experienced younger manager offering them advice. Contracting at the beginning of the relationship can help with this to be sure that both parties understand the 'rules'. Training, matching people and rapport-building sessions can also help, as can a good supervisory process where both the coach and coachee can call upon someone who understands the process to help them should they need it. (More information about coaching supervision can be found in Chapter 27.)

Reverse coaching is really a two-way learning process and both parties must be willing to listen non-judgementally, inquire to hear new ideas, deal with feedback, challenge each other's thinking, be open-minded, show patience and take action. Having a game plan, discussing the rules for the relationship and agreeing a way of working together will be hugely beneficial. Reverse coaching can be both formal or informal. It can be a formal organisation-wide initiative, in which it is more likely that training and guidelines will be offered; or it can be informal, where the two parties simply agree between themselves that they can work together in a mutually satisfying developmental relationship.

Reverse coaching is really a two-way learning process

It's a situation where the old fogies in an organisation realise that by the time you're in your forties or fifties, you are not in touch with the future in the same way as the young twenty somethings are. They come with fresh eyes, open minds and instant links to the technology of our future.

Alan Webber, co-founder of Fast Company

Tips for success

▐ Remember, we can all learn from each other.

▐ Active involvement in reverse coaching can help rid your organisation of complacency.

▐ Paying attention to younger people's challenges and insights will help them to integrate, support talent management and reduce turnover.

Part

5

Final thoughts

In this closing part of the book we offer some final thoughts, ideas and suggestions. We look at coaching supervision, what it is and the role it can play for leaders and managers as coach. We also offer some tips for excellence and some traps to avoid.

27

Coaching supervision

As coaching has grown as a contemporary approach to learning and development, so too has the idea of coaching supervision. Professional coaches in business, leadership, sport and the arts have for many years been encouraged to take part in coaching supervision. Typically they would meet with their supervisor or supervisory group for four or five sessions a year. Other helping professions – such as counsellors and psychotherapists – are also very familiar with this technique as part of their quality and developmental process. Some organisations, which have invested in coaching as one of their major development approaches, have also introduced the idea of supervision into their practice. In this short chapter we will explore what supervision is and why it is important for the coach, coachee and the organisation.

What does coaching supervision involve?

A recent report by the Chartered Institute of Personnel and Development offered the following definition for coaching supervision: '. . . a structured formal process for coaches, with the help of a coaching supervisor, to attend to improving the quality of their coaching, grow their coaching capacity and support themselves and their practice. Supervision should also be a source of organisational learning' (CIPD 2006).

Briefly, coaching supervision is a process whereby a coach or group of coaches have the opportunity, with the help of a coaching supervisor to reflect about their client work in order to develop as a coach. The purpose of this supervision is to learn from their various coaching experiences, to review their practice to ensure they are maintaining their standards and working within ethical parameters, and to provide emotional support to the coach. Supervisors are often a more experienced coach or increasingly someone who has trained as a coaching supervisor. Coaching can be an intense and emotionally draining experience. Having someone to share this with is invaluable for self-protection and quality control.

Coaching can be an intense and emotionally draining experience

In the business environment the idea of 'supervision' can put people off. So some organisations are setting up systems of having a 'lead coach' where they are acting as both a coordinator of coaching within the organisation as well as the go-to person for support and assistance. For others, creating small groups of coaches who undertake regular 'reflective practice' as a form of self-regulation and support is proving popular. Some organisations operate both systems.

For example, at the John Lewis Partnership Steve Ridgley (Coaching Manager) told us that supervision is 'an important part of the internal coaching process'. He went on to explain that it ensures that coaches are supported emotionally, able to share experiences, learn from each other, ensures good quality, and that ethical standards are maintained. All their internal coaches have the opportunity to attend group coaching sessions on a regular basis as well as having the opportunity to have a one to one coaching session if required. At the John Lewis Partnership the supervisors are all internal and have received specialist training to undertake this role. In addition, these supervisors also attend supervision sessions on a regular basis with external supervisors.

One of the challenges for coaching supervision is not breaking any confidences especially when in group supervision sessions. It is, however, possible to talk about an issue that may be bothering you without mentioning names or organisations – the important issue is to be sure you are discrete and yet to be able to share the issue that is challenging you and get support about it so that you can be even more effective in helping your coachee.

> One of the challenges for coaching supervision is not breaking any confidences

Benefits of coaching supervision

The benefits of coaching supervision can be felt by the coach themselves, the people being coached and the organisation. Table 27.1 highlights the benefits.

Setting up and taking part in coaching supervision as part of an organisation's coaching development policy is an example of excellence in coaching practice. Perhaps one of the main benefits for everyone is that the coach feels supported and able to share any issues openly so that they can be the best they can be, and continue to develop and build their capability.

TABLE 27.1 Coaching supervision – the benefits

The coach	The coachee	The organisation
• Helps the coach to be sure they are delivering a quality service	• Gives a sense that the organisation is taking coaching seriously	• Helps ensure that coaches are operating ethically
• Contributes to the coach's personal development	• Provides the knowledge that the coach is well trained and competent	• Helps to assess the benefits of coaching for the organisation and coachee
• Improves the coach's capability and competence	• Reassures that the coach is working within ethical guidelines	• Provides a process for monitoring coaching quality
• Offers the opportunity for self-reflection	• Enables the coach to receive ongoing professional development which benefits the coachee	• Helps the organisation to assess and offer development to their coaches
• Provides the coach with an emotional outlet and an opportunity to explore their feelings in relation to tricky issues		• Can highlight development areas for managers and staff in the organisation
• Enables coaches to learn from each other and build a sense of community		

Features of coaching supervision

There are certain key features of good-quality coaching supervision that you should be aware of as these will contribute to the success of your involvement in the process.

▌ First, it is important that all parties involved are aware of the purpose of the coaching supervision – typically the main reasons for establishing some sort of supervisory process would be:

– To provide a support mechanism for the coach. As coaching can be quite an emotional experience for all involved it is good to have an opportunity to reflect and review for your own self-protection.

— To provide continuing professional development (CPD). Some organisations and professional bodies expect their coaches to take part in this sort of process as part of their CPD and their ongoing involvement as a coach to ensure both quality and ethical standards are being met.

— To identify skill development areas. Sharing your challenges and experiences can lead to awareness that new skills may be necessary.

— To help you spot any organisational learning and development needs. Group supervision or reflective sessions can raise awareness of common issues and can assist an organisation in identifying development needs for their managers and staff.

Second, by establishing a framework to work through during your supervision sessions you will give them purpose and structure. It will also make it easier for the coach to prepare for the sessions. Figure 27.1 sets out what a typical framework might involve.

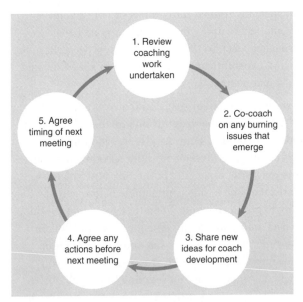

FIGURE 27.1 A framework for coaching supervision

▌ Third, part of any coaching supervision agreement will be to discuss the frequency of the supervision. Some people find that they benefit greatly from regular monthly or bi-monthly meetings, while others want to attend on a needs-only basis. This will very much depend upon the particular individuals and organisations involved. Some organisations make it a condition that all their coaches attend a set number of hours of supervision per year.

▌ Fourth, having clearly established rules of engagement will also help in the process. Regarding confidentiality, for instance, it is important to establish a rule that no names will be mentioned (especially when involved in group supervision within an organisation). Other key rules include the length of time of each meeting, access between meetings, cancellation process, note taking during meetings and maximum numbers at group meetings.

▌ Fifth, any individual or organisation deciding to use coaching supervision as part of their coaching development process will have to decide whether or not to use specially trained individuals or not. Whatever route you decide upon, the supervisor must be an experienced coach in their own right in order to have the skills and capabilities to fulfil the role in a credible and professional manner.

▌ And sixth, a further key decision that you will have to make is whether supervision is one to one or in a group, or indeed it could be both. Any supervision involves the coach opening up their work for scrutiny and some people may find, especially in the first few supervision sessions, that one to one is preferable before perhaps then moving to group coaching when they feel more confident as a coach and with the supervision process. With one to one supervision you have the undivided attention of the supervisor, while with group supervision you have greater opportunity for learning from each other's experience.

Coaching supervision is slowly becoming an accepted part of a coach's development and will certainly highlight the importance of coaching as part of the organisation's development strategy. Coaching is rapidly becoming a popular development technique for many people in organisations. In the most recent Ashridge Management Index (a research project which explores practising managers' attitudes to and experiences of contemporary business life) 72 per cent of respondents felt that they were spending more time coaching their staff, while 77 per cent felt that their own development would benefit from having a coach.

> Coaching is rapidly becoming a popular development technique

If coaching is going to be an element of a leader's or manager's role then it is vital that the quality of the coaching and the skills of the coaches are maintained and developed. One method of doing this is to offer coaching supervision for all who undertake the role of coach.

Tips for success

▌ Take part in coaching supervision to ensure:

– You continue to develop your coaching skills.

– You have the required emotional and practical support.

– You have an outlet to deal with any tricky issues you encounter in your coaching relationships.

– You learn from others who have a similar role to your own.

▌ Taking part in coaching supervision demonstrates that you value ethical principles and quality in your practice.

28

Ten tips for excellence in coaching and mentoring

There are some vital skills and behaviours that contribute to your success as a coach.

- **Listen attentively.** Be sure you hear and fully understand what your coachee is telling you. Listen for what is not being said and above all do not interrupt.

- **Be present and focused.** Ensure that you bring your whole attention and focus to any coaching meeting.

- **Seek to understand and not to judge.** Your role is to maintain an open mind and encourage your coachee to share their feelings, concerns and ideas with you. A coachee will not share if all you do is criticise and judge.

- **Ask open, positive questions.** This will encourage your coachee to explore their issues from every perspective.

- **Be positive.** Look for solutions with the coachee rather than trying to solve the problem for them.

- **Show interest in and empathy for your coachee.** Increasingly the critical success factor is to develop good-quality relationships with your coachees.

- **Help your coachee create specific goals.** They can then have specific outcomes to achieve.

- **Look for the coachee's strengths and successes.** This will help put them in a positive, energetic frame of mind to address whatever issues and concerns they are facing.

- **Keep learning and developing as a coach.** That way you keep up to date with new developments and take account of latest thinking.

- **Demonstrate good ethical practice.** Maintaining confidentiality at all times.

Ten traps to avoid when coaching or mentoring

When you are coaching someone, it is very easy to develop unhelpful behaviours and bad practices. The following are some of the traps you may fall into when coaching – we have seen all of them and fallen into most of them ourselves!

- **Taking the monkey**. There is an expression 'To take the monkey', meaning that you end up taking on other people's problems and issues. This is extremely common in management for two reasons. One, the manager very often thinks that their job is to solve problems; and two, as a result of hierarchy and a command and control culture, many employees have become used to letting someone else do their thinking for them. So as a coach you must avoid taking responsibility for other people's issues. Your job is to make them do the thinking and not solve the problem for them!

- **Giving advice.** In our workshops we observe many examples of managers whose default style is to go immediately to giving advice. What we call the '*Why don't you?*' or '*If I were you*' style of coaching. We know that it is difficult to resist giving advice, and of course sometimes advice is necessary, but it is not coaching! So instead of giving advice, put it aside and tell yourself that you are there to help the coachee find their own answers and use the coaching processes mentioned to focus your mind on getting the coachee to reflect and come up with options.

▌ **Offering a solution.** An employee comes to the manager with an issue and instead of asking questions and listening, the manager feels obliged to offer *their* solution to the employee. Apart from the fact that the boss is not always right, this leads to a mental laziness from the employee, who is not being forced to think the issue through and come up with different courses of action.

▌ **Interrupting.** This is such a common thing for managers to do. Sometimes it comes from arrogance but often it comes from a sense of trying to be helpful. But interrupting people is an insidious thing. People have a basic psychological need to be heard and listened to, and you are denying that if you interrupt them. You are also telling them that their point of view is less important than yours, which is disruptive to the coaching process.

▌ **Not being fully present.** Be fully present and in the moment when you are coaching. It means that the most important thing you can do is give the coachee your presence and full attention. It is not always necessary to know what your next question is in advance, but if you are fully focused on the coachee with your mind firmly in the present, then you will notice more and hear more and your next question will be easier.

▌ **Inappropriate non-verbal behaviour.** Your coachee will be observing you at the same time as you are observing them. This means that you have to pay attention to your own non-verbal behaviour. You need to be able to show interest and energy. Avoid showing any impatience, don't fidget and don't look at your watch during the session, it will just make the coachee feel that they need to hurry up. Remember to set some guidelines about confidentiality and timing at the start of the session to avoid this.

▌ **Being distracted.** This can easily happen. You too have many things on your mind and you can allow your thoughts to wander during the process. This means that you are not focusing on the present situation, not listening closely enough to what is being said and not paying attention to the nuances and changes of tone. You then stay on a superficial level and don't pick up on the underlying issues. Also your coachee will readily notice that you are not paying attention and will conclude that you are not taking them, or the issue – or both – seriously.

▌ **Interrogating.** This can be a risk if the coach starts asking too many closed questions in an impatient and hurried way. The coachee does not feel listened to and feels that the coach is not trying to explore the issue together, but is just looking for facts that could then be used to criticise. You also have to pay attention to your tone of voice. The process can also seem like an interrogation if you are not taking account of the coachee's feelings and emotions.

▌ **Blaming and judging.** If you become critical of the coachee and their actions, and they feel that you are blaming them, it will just make them defensive. The sense that you are being judgemental comes from the words you use of course, but also by the tone of your voice. When coaching someone you must remain open minded, neutral and non-judgemental. You are trying to get at the reality and truth of things, and criticising is the surest way of making the coachee clam up, and you will have achieved nothing.

▌ **Asking leading questions.** As we write in the main body of the book, questioning is one of the key skills of an effective coach. It is as simple as this: '*If you can't ask good questions then you can't be an effective coach.*' One of the common traps we observe is for managers to ask leading questions – that is, questions which lead the coachee into replying in a certain way.

For example questions like, *'Do you think you could help John with that?'* This is basically suggesting that it would be a good idea to help John. And it might well be, but it's not the coachee's idea! Or, *'Don't you agree that this is a good course of action?'* Again this is really suggesting that the coachee agree with you that it is a good course of action. The danger then is that the coachee just says yes it is, but actually is not really committed to that particular action. Or, *'How did you feel about that – angry?'* This is limiting the coachee's options and the result is that he or she won't do the necessary thinking about what it is that they do feel.

Don't worry if you have fallen into some or all of these traps, most coaches do at some time. The essential thing is to be aware of your mistakes and ensure you learn from them.

Conclusion

In recent years there has been much research about the use and impact of coaching as a development process in organisations. We have outlined some of the research in this book and it is clear from that research that you as a leader or manager are going to need to be able to adopt a coaching style of management. Looking forward, it is becoming evident that a coaching style will become THE definitive approach to leading and managing.

We hope that this book will have convinced you of the need to coach and will accompany you on your journey to being a leader as coach. You will be amazed at the benefits not just for the people you coach, but also for yourself and your organisation.

We hope you enjoyed the book and we wish you the very best of luck.

What did you think of this book?

We're really keen to hear from you about this book, so that we can make our publishing even better.

Please log on to the following website and leave us your feedback.

It will only take a few minutes and your thoughts are invaluable to us.

www.pearsoned.co.uk/bookfeedback

Coaching resources

- Professional bodies
  - European Mentoring and Coaching Council
  - International Coach Federation
  - Association for Coaching UK
  - The Association for Professional Executive Coaches
- Qualification programmes
  - Masters in Executive Coaching – Ashridge Business School
  - MSc Career Management and Coaching – Birkbeck College
  - MA Coaching and Mentoring Practice – Oxford Brooks University
  - MSc Coaching and Behavioural Change – Henley Business School
- Short course providers
  - Ashridge Business School
  - City University
  - Chartered Institute of Personnel and Development
  - Management Futures

References

Akabussi, K. (2014) Personal conversation with authors.

Berg, I. K. and Szabo, P. (2005) *Brief Coaching For Lasting Solutions*. Norton.

Bharucha, K. (2013) *How to get Coaching Right*. Corporate Executive Board.

BNP Paribas (2015) *La Grande InvaZion*. The Boston Project.

Bowden, M. (2012) *The Finish*. Atlantic Books.

Bowring, K. interview at RFU HQ Twickenham 8 July 2014.

Brent, M. and Dent, F. E. (2014) *The Leaders Guide to Managing People: How to use soft skills to get hard results*. Pearson.

Cappelli, P., Singh, H., Singh, J. V. and Useem, M. (2010) 'Leadership Lessons From India'. *Harvard Business Review*, March.

Chartered Institute of Personnel and Development [CIPD] (2013) *Learning and Talent Development Annual Survey*.

Chartered Institute of Personnel and Development [CIPD] (2011) *The Coaching Climate*.

Chartered Institute of Personnel and Development [CIPD] (2009) *Taking the Temperature of Coaching*.

Chartered Institute of Personnel and Development [CIPD] (2008) *Engaging Leadership: Creating Organisations That Maximise the Potential of Their People*.

Chartered Institute of Personnel and Development [CIPD] (2006). *Change Agenda: Coaching Supervision Maximising the Potential of Coaching*.

Clutterbuck, D. (2007) *Coaching the Team at Work*. Nicholas Brearley Publishing.

Clutterbuck, D. (1995) *Mentoring In Action: A Practical Guide for Managers*. Kogan Page.

Clutterbuck, D. and Megginson, D. (2004). *Techniques For Coaching and Mentoring*. Routledge.

Cooperrider, D. and Whitney, D. (2005) *Appreciative Inquiry: A Positive Revolution in Change*. Berrett-Koehler.

Covey, S. (2006) *The Speed of Trust*. Simon Schuster.

Davies, S. (2012) *Embracing Reflective Practice. Education For Primary Care*. Radcliffe Publishing.

De Haan, E. (2012) *Supervision In Action: A relational approach to coaching and consulting supervision*. Open University Press.

De Haan, E. and Burger, Y. (2013) *Coaching with Colleagues: An action guide for one to one learning*. Palgrave MacMillan.

Dembkowski, S. and Eldridge, F. (2003) 'Beyond GROW: A new coaching model'. *The International Journal of Mentoring and Coaching*, Vol. 1, No. 1, November.

Dent, F. E. (2009) *Working Relationships Pocketbook*. Management Pocketbooks.

Dent, F., Paine Schofield, C. and Holton, V. (2010) *The Ashridge Management Index*. Ashridge Business School.

Dent, F., Rabbetts, J. and Holton, V. (2013) *The Ashridge Management Index*. Ashridge Business School.

De Rond, M. (2012) *There is an I in Team: What elite athletes and coaches really know about high performance*. Harvard Business Publishing.

Downey, M. (2003) *Effective Coaching Lessons from the Coaches Coach*. Thomson Texere.

Firth, D. (1998) *The Corporate Fool*. Capstone.

Grint, K. (2005) *Leadership: Limits and Possibilities*. Palgrave MacMillan.

Hall, E. (1998) *The Hidden Dimension*. Doubleday.

Hardingham, A., with Brearley, M., Moorhouse, A. and Venter, B. (2004) *The Coach's Coach: Personal development for personal developers*. Chartered Institute of Personnel and Development.

Hawkins, P. (2014) *Leadership Team Coaching in Practice*. Kogan Page.

Hawkins, P. and Smith, N. (2006) *Coaching, Mentoring and Organisational Consultancy: Supervision and Development*. Oxford University Press.

Heron, J. (2001) *Helping The Client: A Creative Practical Guide*. Sage Publications.

Hofstede, G., et al. (2011) *Cultures and Organisations: Software of the Mind*. McGraw Hill.

Honore, S. and Paine Schofield, C. (2012) *Culture Shock: Generation Y and Their Managers Round The World*. Ashridge Business School.

Honore, S. and Paine Schofield, C. (2011) *Great Expectations: Managing Generation Y*. Ashridge Business School and Institute of Leadership and Management.

Kessler, E. H. (ed.) (2013) *Encyclopaedia of Management Theory*. Sage Publications.

Jackson, P. Z. and McKergow, M. (2011) *Solutions Focus: Making Coaching and Change SIMPLE*. Nicholas Brealey Publishing.

Mehrabian, A. (1981) *Silent Messages: Implicit Communication of Emotions and Attitudes*. Belmont, CA: Wadsworth.

Meister, G. and Willyard, K. (2010) *Mentoring Mill*. Harvard Business Review.

Melville, N. (2014) Personal conversation with authors.

Palmer, S. (2007) 'PRACTICE: A model suitable for coaching, counselling, psychotherapy and stress management'. *The Coaching Psychologist*, Vol. 3, No. 2, 71–77.

Parsloe, E. (1999) *The Manager as Coach and Mentor*. CIPD.

Pink, D. (2010) *Drive: The Simple Truth About What Motivates Us*. Canongate Books.

Revans, R. (2011) *The ABC of Action Learning*. Gower.

Ridler (2013) *Trends in the Use of Executive Coaching*. Ridler and Co and EMCC.

Rittel, H. and Webber, M. (1973) 'Dilemmas in a General Theory of Planning'. *Policy Sciences*, Vol. 4, 155–169.

Rogers, C. (1951) *Client-Centred Therapy: Its current practice, implications and theory*. Constable.

Rogers, J. (2004) *Coaching Skills: A Handbook*. Open University Press.

Stacey, R. (1996) *Complexity and Creativity in Organisations*. Berret-Koehler.

Toffler, A. (1999) *Future Shock*. Turtleback Books.

Wasik, B. (1984) 'Teaching parents effective problem-solving: A handbook for professionals'. Unpublished manuscript. Chapel Hill: University of North Carolina.

Whitmore, J. (2010) *Coaching For Performance: GROWing Human Potential and Purpose: The Principles and Practice of Coaching and Leadership*. Nicholas Brealey Publishing.

Index